C

PART 1:
THE HIGH CALL OF MANLINESS

PART 2:
THE 5 PRINCIPLES OF LIVING MANFULLY

Tending THE FIRE

MIKE YARBROUGH

I dedicate this book to my sons and their fire within.

PROLOGUE

THANKSGIVING DAY, 2019: 9:00 A.M.

Nearly every Thanksgiving of my life, and likely yours as well, has been spent with family or friends. Typically, I wake early to cook all of the usuals: turkey, ham, a special stuffing, rolls, and all of the fixings, with the house still filled with the sweet aroma of pies prepared the night before.

Though I like to think of Thanksgiving as a day of feasting, it's more like a day of preparing followed by an all too brief moment of stuffing ourselves and then watching in sorrow as the leftovers get sent home with the guests. But it's worth it. Every year.

This Thanksgiving, however, for the first time in my life, I was alone.

My wife Summer and I were two months into a nasty separation. Not feeling welcomed in my own home and not wanting to bring any drama to our friends on a holiday, I decided to drive to the small town of Black Mountain, North Carolina—about an hour and a half from my home in Charlotte—to spend the day hiking and in contemplation of how we arrived at this place in our marriage.

Had twenty-three years of hard-fought marriage and raising our boys together really come to this? I wondered. *How many more Thanksgivings and holidays will look just like this one?*

To be honest, this isn't how I intended to open this book. When I first sat down to pen this tome, I imagined an introduction of such inspiring eloquence that men across the globe would take hold of the words contained herein and move upon their world like a sort of possessed orchestra—loud and thundering, yet with a beautiful harmony in the midst of it all.

But the truth is, there are a lot of things in my life that haven't gone as intended. Instead, I've brought a bit of my own story and my own fire to these pages—the real stuff. This is where the heart is, and, thus, where *my heart* is. I'm bringing you in close so that you might catch a genuine flame rather than an impersonal ideal.

There's a High Calling upon the life of a man. For some, the call is a whisper. For others, it beckons boldly: put the world in order, reject the status quo, live with passion, do what matters, and protect what you love.

The problem is, if we hear this High Call of manliness and yet lack the skills to live it out, we'll fail ourselves. And when we face disappointments in life, we can begin to feel ashamed and defeated. Over time we become reluctant to swing for the fences.

That's what I was feeling, that lonely Thanksgiving morning.

9:45 A.M.

On that solitary Thanksgiving morning, halfway to Black Mountain, I called home. The feelings of loneliness and the pain of holidays without my family made me look past the feelings of exasperation and defeat in my marriage. This was a fire tending moment for me.

To call home and let the longings of my heart be known without any certainty as to what would happen next was a challenge for a lone wolf. The truth is, I am a man that needs his family and longs for a community. This means there are desires of my heart that can only be satisfied by someone else. Opening myself up to this truth also meant facing the possibility of rejection. There's an uncomfortable vulnerability in making our deepest desires known. And that's exactly what I did.

One way or another, this call was going to be a defining moment.

Fortunately, my wife Summer heard the tenderness in my voice and responded in kind. My marriage wasn't going to end. In fact, this was the beginning of a new and much happier chapter in our lives.

My friend Stephen Mansfield played a role in saving my marriage. Just a few weeks earlier, Stephen and I had a chance to sit down at a men's retreat in Black Mountain. I'd read a number of his books (as should you) and interviewed him on my podcast some time before. Though I was intent on talking shop about the state of manhood and book publishing, he drew me out. Before I knew it, the story of my separation was on the table. In his fatherly way, he asked questions and listened to me as I laid it all out.

Despite my obvious feelings of finality to my marriage, he encouraged me: "Mike, I don't believe your marriage is over. I believe there's still hope."

No one wants to disappoint the hope of a man they admire.

My fire was burning low, and Mansfield's much-needed hope was a bit of timber from a friend.

Tending the fire of our souls can be like that. As Mansfield writes in his book, *Men on Fire*, "Once an ignition has occurred, protect the fire, feed the fire and tend it as you must so it will engulf your heart." Once you know the principles that ignite your heart, you can help your brothers do the same.

As you may have guessed, I don't have it all figured out. I'm on the journey toward becoming a better man. I've traveled some unsteady roads, made a few good turns over rough terrain, and I've found there are certain principles that keep us on the right path. They're maxims of masculinity that'll light our fires and help us find our way through the darkness.

In the six years since I started writing this book my life has been filled with unexpected challenges and blessings. I've grown a movement for men called Wolf & Iron, wrote a little book about pocketknives, saw my sons graduate high school, launched a successful business with my wife making wedding rings from historic woods, watched my dad take his last breaths, and scattered his ashes on a mountain far from home.

At each twist and turn of life, the principles in this book have guided me. They've proven to be a trustworthy foundation upon which to stand.

Friend, if you're ready to ignite your heart and truly live life as a man, read on.

INTRODUCTION

What is to give light must endure burning.

VICTOR FRANKL, AUTHOR, PSYCHIATRIST, AND HOLOCAUST SURVIVOR

Imagine with me if you will. You are alone, in deep woods, with a great canopy of green and brown overhead. The canopy of trees pushing back all the world and embracing only a single man: you. The sun never beats down here, if there is sun. And while I suppose you could determine whether it were the moon or the sun that illumes the grandeur above and pours out soft and white through the fog onto the forest floor, you would never strain to do so here. You have not come to analyze but to tend, and the forest needs no tending.

You stand in a clearing and *your* fire is before you—its ashes spread wide within a circle of large stones that mark its boundary. These stones, did you bring them to this place? No, you did not. How could you? See how they disappear into the earth? How deep they must go. They're beautiful and immovable and in their center burns an earnest flame.

Now, the fire is nothing to brag about, but it's hardy enough. It's the type of flame that keeps the chill off most nights, though, you say to yourself, '*Perhaps not this night.*' It's early, and already a cool breeze has taken up and seems to have found its home in the ground. Your lower extremities are telling the rest of your body that *the cold is coming*. You instinctively know you must keep moving and tend your fire.

To your left is a crude but sturdy lean-to that serves as an entryway to a great cave. The scant covering is moss-covered and old, and, while it may be more ornamental than practical, it softens the appearance of the cave. Did you make this lean-to? Yes.

Outside the mouth of the cave, under the lean-to, you have staged the fuel for your fire. Stacks of old, worn, and faceless books, newspapers, and magazines are housed in broken and discarded boxes. There is some wood as well—sticks really—soft and unseasoned. It's the type of wood that hisses and pops when it burns and wakes you in the night.

You peer into the cave and its darkness overwhelms the flicker of light behind you. Within lies more fuel for your fire. The more intently you stare into the cave the more the outside begins to fade into the dim, and in a moment all you see is black. You have been in the cave many times but never deeply. If the swallowing darkness of the cavern wasn't enough to keep you from venturing further in, the tales of what lies beyond—recounted to you from boyhood—will and do.

Is it even necessary to venture deep into the cave? Near the entrance, stacks of boxes are filled with more old books and papers. They're light and easy to carry, and they catch flame quite effortlessly. But, they're quickly consumed, and on a cold night there's no rest. Always, you are waking and heaving handfuls and armfuls into that great furnace; tonight, perhaps, boxfuls.

You make your way back to the fire and toss in some old books. They quickly catch and their brief flash of heat rebukes the chill in the air, but they are fast consumed, and the cold comes on again. As you reach for another armful, something in the distance catches your eye. There, through the trees, you see a glimmer and now a glow.

You steady yourself to be sure of what you are seeing and then you realize—it is the fire of another man. How can this be? It seems miles away from you. How could anyone stand a fire so intense? *This fool must have thrown all of his books on his fire at once.* You sit and watch for a while. His fire grows and fades—appearing so faint that your eyes can no longer focus—and then reappears bright and steady.

But how could someone keep it going for so long with such intensity? Perhaps his cave is nearer to his fire? Perhaps his books are somehow different. Or he can carry more. Or he's faster than me.

Then a new thought forms.

Perhaps he has found what burns, deep in his cave.

The Fire of Man

I have inside information about you. As a man who also possesses the mighty Y chromosome, I have first-hand knowledge of the inner workings of a man. Over the years I've found that we men are alike in many ways.

Certainly, you and I are alike in many ways that matter most. As men, I believe we have a fire within us that needs to be tended. In fact, it must be tended. If we neglect the fire within us, we'll never become the men we ought to be.

Plato and Socrates called this inner man the *psyche,* but in western culture we know it better as the soul or the heart of a man. It is both our lifeforce and our passion for living; our vim and vigor. It is our full being—the representation of our abstract self. It's who we are aside from our body and physical limitations. For some of us it may be, as Jack London described it in *White Fang*, "a secret prompting, an urge of instinct." It's where we feel that nagging discontentment that points us towards something greater.

In other words, there's a fire in each of our souls in need of those long-burning hardwoods—hickory and oak. The problem is, the souls of most men are only getting paper, pine, and shrubs. It's poor fuel for any aspect of life that requires a man to be successful: fatherhood, being a leader in your own home, standing up for what you believe in, physical strength, and hard, rewarding work. The fuel of modern life is inadequate for a man of conviction and action.

If you're feeling that nagging sense of discontentment and craving fuel that satisfies your heart, this book is for you.

The Cavern of Our Soul

Perhaps it's etched into us from our earliest days of seeking shelter and community, but the image of a cave seems to appear quite naturally when speaking on the inner workings of a man. In the years since writing this book, I've seen this allegory show up in the books of some of my favorite authors. However, because we have something of an instinctual understanding of the cave, we rarely define what it represents.

In the time of our great ancestors, a cave represented shelter and security. It held the promise of survival and the continuance of a family bloodline. However, before one could settle into a cave, one had to face the darkness therein and it was quite possible that some deadly creature had already taken up residence. In order for a man to make a home for his family, he would need to drive out any current inhabitants.

It was a risk, and some of us are here today because a man took that risk, and won.

But there is something else to be found in the cave which is not to be feared. Something which gives life and can only be discovered by venturing into the darkness and facing whatever lies in wait.

Courage. Boldness. Hardihood. Honor. Pride.

They are the timbers of old, felled before our time, and ready to fuel the fire of our soul. And there are others like it, deeper within the cave.

If there are aspects of yourself that feel dark and unexplored, yet yearn to be known, keep reading. This book is for you.

I'm going to help you lay a foundation in your mind and heart that will help you become the kind of man you want to be. The kind of man that's so desperately needed in this modern age, just as it's been needed in every age throughout history. A man who knows the inner workings of his heart and fights for the goodness hidden there. A man who tends his fire and inspires other men to do the same.

Part 1

THE HIGH CALL OF MANLINESS

1

THE PROBLEM

A Lack of Manhood

We need the iron qualities that go with true manhood. We need the positive virtues of resolution, of courage, of indomitable will, of power to do without shrinking the rough work that must always be done.

THEODORE ROOSEVELT,
ROUGH RIDER, AUTHOR, BOXER, AND MAN

It's interesting how words change over time. Take for example the word *gentleman*. In the Middle Ages it meant someone was a landed noble—a landed *gentry*. To say, "There goes a gentleman" was to say there goes someone who owns land from which he makes a living.

To say that someone wasn't a gentleman was considered a fact, not an insult. Yet over time, well-meaning people, or perhaps a poet, decided that being a gentleman was more of a heart attitude which could be reflected by any man with the character traits of a noble person. Today, you can be a gentleman by simply holding the door open for a lady or just being a kind-hearted man. I suppose the transformation of this word isn't a loss for society, but it is a loss for the word itself. The term floats around with no apparent structure or definitive meaning.

The same is true for what it means to be a *man*.

If we asked people 100 years ago what it meant to be a man, we would no doubt be inspired by their responses. It was the highest honor a person could receive. It was a culmination of a person's character, physical and emotional strength, intellect, wisdom, and humility. To live as a man—or to live manfully—would've been well understood. It was to live in such a way that all of the great traits of a man were sought out like treasure. To take up the High Call of manliness was a noble act in and of itself. And to show character that was unmanly was despised.

However, being a man has undergone a change of meaning in modern society. Now it's used interchangeably with *macho* or bound to tropes and stereotypes of men as buffoons. Like the word gentleman, it's used wherever it feels right, to the point of uselessness.

Though I don't believe this change has come about as a conspiracy or a direct attack on what it means to be a man, I do believe there are groups that truly hate men. While I'm sure those groups do some damage, I don't think that's the cause of the emasculation and dumbing down of men we see today. Instead, redefining what it means to be a man has to do with the ridiculous amount of time in which we are being sold to throughout our day.

Never before in history has a people been so completely enveloped in a world designed to sell to them as we are today. Almost all of our recreational time, heck, almost all of our waking hours that we're not sitting alone, reading a book, or talking with a friend, we are being sold to. Radio, TV, movies, internet, mobile devices, games—advertisements are everywhere. Advertisements aren't only constant during almost all of our waking hours, but they also come in short bursts.

They're designed to attract our attention and tell a story in a very short amount of time. As a result, they drive so many of the anti-manly—as well as anti-womanly or one-dimensional woman—stereotypes we see today.

For instance, a man who's a man in the traditional sense—a man who is too busy to get caught up in stupid arguments, doesn't find himself in foolhardy situations, and has a certainty and purpose about his life—this kind of guy doesn't provide a lot of fodder for a quick story. This is why jokes don't start with, "A good and honest man walks into a bar." In any good story there must be a conflict of sorts that needs to be solved. In most commercials and TV shows, a man's conflict is often with his own foolishness because it's the easiest conflict to create. Therefore, we're now barraged on every front with a fictitious world filled with spineless buffoons who only care about beer, boobs, and bacon.

At one point this was new and rather clever. In the 1940s and 1950s, advertisements portrayed men as heroes. Fathers were shown as the ultimate role model and authority figure. Kids would tune in on their radios to hear broadcasts of Sherlock Holmes, Detective Sam Spade, or cowboys like Roy Rogers and Hopalong Cassidy. The accounts of the heroic acts of World War I and World War II were told by the returning heroes themselves.

It's easy to see, then, how advertisements that began to appear in the late 1950s and 1960s—advertisements that poked fun at men or portrayed them in a non-heroic light—would've stood out and appealed to women who were becoming part of the workforce. Seeing a man in the kitchen, wearing an apron, and doing dishes? That really got the viewer's attention! Showcasing men as helpless, distemperate buffoons was a true marketing disruptor. Unfortunately, advertisers are still using this formula, and generations of men and women have had their concepts of manhood shaped by media more so than family, friends, and heroes.

The point isn't that we should do away with these kinds of portrayals of men but that we simply have too much of the same narrative. True manliness has been out of public view for so long that people can't call to mind what it even looks like. This allows for the common narrative to fill in the gap.

The question then is, how would our world fare differently if men showed up as men in the various areas of life?

HEALTH: OBESITY, THE COST OF HEALTHCARE, & OUR DEPENDENCE ON MEDICATION

Perfect health is a consciousness of full vitality, of exhilaration, keen enjoyment of life, and strength to perform any task, and it is a melancholy reflection that not one in a thousand men and women of middle-age has it.

EUGEN SANDOW, THE GOSPEL OF STRENGTH

There's a large movement—particularly among young people—toward natural medicine and caring for their bodies through diet and exercise before going to the doctor. Many of them feel they're being forced into an outdated system of insurance or government-mandated healthcare in which they're required to subsidize the cost of others to avoid a tax penalty at the end of the year.

This isn't a political point I'm trying to make. It's a practical one. Those young people have the right idea, and it's a very manly idea: take responsibility for your health.

As a nation, we have an obesity epidemic. Obesity has soared from 13 percent of the population in 1960 to nearly 40 percent in 2016.[1]

1. https://ftp.cdc.gov/pub/Health_Statistics/NCHS/NHIS/SHS/2015_SHS_Table_A-15.pdf

Obesity is not only one of the most serious health issues we're dealing with as a society, but also one of the most embarrassing. I don't mean it's embarrassing from a vanity standpoint, as in we look terrible when we're at the beach. It's embarrassing because it's an issue of self-control and self-will.

Our obesity epidemic says, "When comfort and ease and quick food are so readily available, we don't have the willpower to reject it and manage our own health. Our desire for ease is greater than our desire for a healthy life." That's not a manly way of thinking. That is short-term, satisfaction-now thinking. A man looks at how he's living his life and how it will affect not only him but also his children and grandchildren. And then he takes action to make certain he's moving in the right direction.

The truth is, societal change begins with each of us men looking at the man in the mirror and taking responsibility for the person staring back. The man who accepts responsibility for his own life lives in moderation and denies himself momentary pleasures because he loves the feeling of doing what's right. He settles his will against his appetitive nature. And while he may not be victorious at every turn, he will put up one hell of a fight.

So how does manly living address the cost of healthcare? Each one of us must take responsibility for his own diet and fitness to reduce the need for doctors. We must also stop seeking a pill for every little issue. And we need to start paying doctors directly for their services to save insurance for what it's really for. With a serious recommitment to physical culture and a patient-to-physician relationship, we can drastically change how this conversation looks in fifteen years.

At this point you may be thinking, "That sounds ideal, but is it practical? I mean, can we trust people to take care of themselves?" Men, the reason we have any doubt is because we know ourselves all too well.

We know the temptations we face daily. That is why we must raise the bar and our expectations—first for ourselves but also for the generations to come.

If we're not man enough to take up a solution where the only requirement is to care for our bodies and act responsibly, we're in a sad state indeed.

THE POOR AND FATHERLESS

In what condition is a man to fight for prosperity when he has lost confidence in his ability, and is convinced that opportunity is for others and not for him? He does not believe he can push away the limitations which hedge him in. So he still thinks poverty, talks poverty, acts poverty, dreams poverty, and then wonders why he is unlucky.

ORISON SWETT MARDEN, EVERY MAN A KING

Before I jump into how manliness deals with poverty, let's make sure we're on the same page about what poverty is and what it isn't. In 2012 the U.S. Census[2] reported that poverty affected 15 percent of the population. According to the U.S. Census, poverty is determined by household income and it's roughly a single person making less than $12,000 a year or a family of four making less than $25,000.

Though I understand how this data is helpful for the Census Bureau and politicians, I don't think that necessarily qualifies as poor in all cases. I've heard many people say they didn't have any money growing up, yet never once thought of themselves as poor. They were obviously poor as defined and labeled by the U.S. Census Bureau, but they didn't feel poor because they had everything they needed.

2. https://www.cbpp.org/research/census-data-show-poverty-and-inequality-remained-high-in-2012-and-median-income-was#:~:text=The%20poverty%20rate%20remained%20unchanged,by%20a%20number%20of%20measures.

If you can take care of yourself and you choose to live a simple life under the poverty threshold, you're not poor. If you lack the knowledge or means to provide for yourself and you're in a constant state of need, you're poor. True poverty is to be in a situation where you're unable to provide food, clothing, utilities, education, and medical care for yourself and your family.

There was a time when poor people could lease some land, raise a few animals, farm, and live a simple life. Then their children could either leave the farm or stick around to help provide for the family, slowly bringing the entire family out of poverty and into better days. Some of the best leaders in our nation's history came from this very structure. Somehow, though, our nation's poor are now stuck in urban areas where farming is unheard of and dependence upon subsidies is all too common. Today, self-reliance and the independent spirit that makes for great men is a foreign concept for most people in poverty.

It should also be noted that the average American household has a great deal of debt that isn't taken into account by the poverty estimates of the U.S. Census Bureau. As of March 2020, the average household carries a credit card debt of $6,591, a mortgage debt of $195,967, a student loan debt of $46,954, and auto loan debts of $27,978.[3] I have first-hand experience with this kind of debt, and it can make a man feel poor even though he's making a good income.

Fatherhood and Poverty

The first way manliness addresses poverty is for a man to be present in the family. A 2016 report from the U.S. Census Bureau shows that around 23 percent of American children are fatherless.[4] In 1960 it was

3. https://www.nerdwallet.com/blog/average-credit-card-debt-household/

4. https://www.census.gov/newsroom/press-releases/2016/cb16-192.html

8 percent. That's over sixteen million children who don't know what it's like to have a masculine presence at home each day.

When we take a closer look at the statistics, we see the devastating effects of fatherless homes. Fatherless homes are responsible for 90 percent of runaways, 63 percent of youth suicides, 85 percent of children with behavior disorders, 75 percent of children with chemical abuse, 85 percent of youths in prison, and 70 percent of children in state-operated institutions. All of these factors contribute to poverty. More importantly, they contribute to so many of the god-awful societal issues we witness each day.

The next time you hear about some punk getting busted for a disgusting crime, you know there's a good chance there wasn't a dad in the home. The next time you watch the news cover a murder in a poor area, see if they find any men to interview. Chances are they won't, because they're not there. In many cases, if those families had a man who did nothing but walk through the door each day, those terrible events would have never happened. When there's a man in the home who is growing in character and teaching his children to do the same, a man who is ashamed of any dependence on government or charities to sustain his family, and a man who strives towards independence, it will raise a family out of poverty and all of its devastating effects.

Fellas, let's take a moment to thank the men who are active fathers and husbands. I got married when I was eighteen and I've been with my wife, Summer, ever since. It hasn't always been an easy road. There have been times when the only thing that kept us together was our commitment to each other before God. I know how tough marriage can be—particularly when society begs us to leave our responsibilities and continue in our boyhood pursuits for the remainder of our years.

So, I want to say *thank you* for being the kind of man who does what is right. I hope you realize just how important your commitment to your family is. The choices you make and the lessons you teach are helping to stem the tide of societal collapse. It's no less important than that.

You and your family also serve as a light to countless children who will never know what a family with a father looks like. To you it may seem ordinary, scarcely worth the thought. But to the fatherless, it's a striking and mighty call to goodness.

POLITICAL INVERTEBRATES AND THE RULING CLASS

Everything is changing. People are taking their comedians seriously and the politicians as a joke.

WILL ROGERS,
HUMORIST AND SOCIAL COMMENTATOR

There was a time—albeit early in our American history—when we called upon our finest men to represent us in office: war heroes, inventors, idealists, writers, and orators. Men of notable achievements who deserved respect prior to pursuing any official title or office. It was well known that there would be those who would seek power and wealth at the expense of our freedom, so they elected brilliant and tested men to the highest levels of government.

For several decades we've been sold our politicians—particularly our presidents—rather than choosing them from amongst ourselves. Regardless of political party, the political conventions where presidential and vice-presidential candidates were once fought for and chosen, have now become taxpayer-funded marketing ploys.

Washington and local governments have become so well known for their corruption, mountains of bureaucracy, and layers of red tape, that there are few good men and women who want to leave their private lives to serve the public good. This leaves the political positions open for those who pine for status and control. The result is that we have untested men and women in politics who have not spent their lives resisting temptation, standing firm on principles, and innovating. We have those who excel at simply playing the game of politics.

The Independent Spirit of a Man

The independent, can-do spirit of a man is something that many men are lacking today. What if the men of our nation tended the fire of independence? What difference would it make?

For starters, more men would be qualified to lead in our government. A man who thinks independently thinks for himself, stands by himself, looks to no one else to solve his problems, and expects everyone else to do the same.

Second, men of the independent mindset would look to solve their own problems rather than looking to the government for solutions. They would send leaders to Washington to keep big government out of their lives. As President James A. Garfield said, "*The role of government is to keep the peace, and stand out of the sunshine of the people.*"

Imagine for a moment a nation of men with a well-honed spirit of independence who were beholden to no one but themselves and their own ideals. Imagine those kinds of men running for office with a campaign slogan, "*Here's who I am and what I believe. Take it or leave it.*" Even if you and I didn't agree with that guy, we could respect him more than someone pandering to their party or special interest. That kind of respect for our leaders would change the dialogue across party lines both in Washington and on Main Street.

The spirit of independence doesn't mean self-contained, unattached men who refuse help from anyone ever, although that kind of man can certainly be a welcome citizen. I mean there's a spirit of a man that wants to be tested, to find his limits, take care of himself and his loved ones, and limit the burden of his life on others.

SCHOOL VIOLENCE

Little progress can be made by merely attempting to repress what is evil. Our great hope lies in developing what is good.

CALVIN COOLIDGE, 30TH U.S. PRESIDENT

When we look at the lives and character of our children we can learn a great deal about the track society is on, because the values of a society are evident in its children. As unlearned, empty vessels they adopt the prevalent opinion of the day like sponges rather than forming their own opinions and choosing their own lifestyle.

Are the children of our nation bright and intelligent, growing in wisdom, respectful of themselves and others, and concerned with honor and integrity? If so, you and I can thank adults because we're the ones instilling these qualities in our children.

Or are the children of our country disrespectful, antagonistic, dull-witted, lazy, and selfish? Once again, the credit or blame for the character of our children lies with our fellow Americans.

What are we to learn, then, if the children of our country are becoming increasingly violent? What if a growing number of them want to kill each other? Can there be a greater red flag for us?

School shootings have been around since there were classrooms and gunpowder. However, there's been an alarming increase in the number of school shootings and mass killings since the 1980s. While the number of killings has increased, the age of the shooters has decreased, and the nature of the shootings has changed. There are more children being killed by other children who feel unloved and outcast by society.

For some, the answer is to grab all of the guns and put police in our schools.

We should never settle on a solution that involves our children going through metal detectors and having their backpacks inspected just to go to school. That should have never become the norm in our society. Our places of education are starting to resemble institutions rather than schoolhouses.

Men, red flags are meant to warn us. We need men to step up and bring a good deal of manliness into our homes and the lives of our children.

Manliness in the Home

Personal moral failings must be addressed individually, starting with you and me. We cannot expect personal morality to be corrected by a public system. The often overlooked, but quite keen, President Calvin Coolidge once said, "Duty is not collective. It is personal."

The rise in school violence cannot be deterred by the school systems alone. If we continue to see school violence as a failure of the system rather than a failure of parents, we will continue to look to the system for solutions. We will look to the things that a system may be able to control: medications, violent video games and movies, and access to guns or other weapons. If we're putting our hope into the system for the solution, then our anger, time, and energy will be directed towards those things. In other words, we will continue to focus on controlling evil rather than developing what is good.

Most problems in society can be traced back to problems in the home. If a child is able to amass a collection of guns and ammo, they are not being parented. If a child posts a video of themselves on YouTube talking about how they hate society and want to kill people and themselves, they are not being parented.

A man takes responsibility for his home. He knows what his children are going through in life and takes action to direct them to the right path. The Bible says, "Raise up a child in the way he should go." This is a directive to action, not perfection. No parent can be aware of everything happening in their home, but we must understand that where abdication of responsibility exists, opportunity for evil also exists.

This goes against so much of what we hear today. Society tells us kids ought to be autonomous. What nonsense!

Men, we must raise our children well. The call to be a father is one of the highest callings you and I have. When we answer the call, we will develop the good in our children.

Manliness in the Classroom

As of 2018, less than 25 percent of the teachers in the U.S. were men.[5] For most boys, that means the majority of their productive hours will be spent taking instructions from a female. We are missing an opportunity to impart some manliness into our sons during the most formative times in their lives.

For a boy, just having a man in the room changes things. It steadies their thoughts and fixes them on both their performance and the man's approval. A boy sees a man as a mentor whereas he sees a woman

5. https://nces.ed.gov/programs/coe/indicator_clr.asp#:~:text=See%20Digest%20of%20Education%20Statistics,school%20level%20(36%20percent).

as a teacher. Men have the ability to draw a young man towards manhood, whereas women—all good intentions aside—have the unfortunate effect of pushing. Parents see this in the home all the time. The mother may have to yell while dad can just give a look or a stern command. This isn't meant to disregard the wonderful influence and building up of young men that women have done and will continue to do. But it's foolish to not recognize and take advantage of the natural characteristics of male relationships.

Would a young man be less likely to start an assault on a school that had a strong male presence? I think so. I believe men are more likely to relate to and befriend a male student. It should be apparent that the young men who are committing these heinous acts are not being parented well. A positive male influence in their lives could have made all the difference because boys generally want to win the approval of men.

It's not surprising when you think about our level of loneliness, isolation, and mission-less existence that we've forgotten the power of influence males have on each other's lives. To prevent loneliness and isolation it's an absolute necessity to have shoulder-to-shoulder interaction, shared risks and challenges, and hard-won victories within a brotherhood. Many men—myself included because I grew up rather isolated—missed out on the opportunity to form those critical emotional and neurological foundations of team and community, so we often don't realize what we're missing until well into adulthood.

When positive male influences are modeled in our lives from an early age, it makes a tremendous difference in our lives going forward.

2

MANLINESS

The Cure for What Ails Us

A blazing fire makes flame and brightness out of everything that is thrown into it.

MARCUS AURELIUS, ROMAN EMPEROR AND STOIC PHILOSOPHER

We need more good men in the world. Perhaps you've had the same thought after reading about a rare heroic act in the news: *We need more men like that.*

No doubt many single women would agree that a good man is hard to find, particularly when they find themselves settling for the best of the bad options that are available. Time and again they witness the drama that unfolds in the lives of their girlfriends as another guy dumps them, cheats on them, won't commit to them, or simply doesn't measure up to the character of an adult, much less a man. In some ways, all of these character flaws are counterfeit masculinity, showing once again that we have dwarfed the standard of what it means to be a man.

When Bill Clinton had his infamous affair with Monica Lewinsky, the women I talked to would say things like, "He's a man, and we all know what men do." Or "Men can't help it, it's what they are programmed to do."

I remember saying, "Really? You're giving this guy a pass? You think all men cheat and are physically and emotionally incapable of being faithful?"

It didn't take long to find out that many of these women had also been hurt by unfaithful men. Perhaps, in order to remove the guilt and responsibility they felt when their man left them, they bought into the lie that men were simply following an involuntary urge of instinct.

Men, this is important. Whenever there's a scandal of infidelity or abuse of power, where are the men who stayed faithful to their wives who stand in direct contrast to what these women believe? The men who keep the oath they swore before their friends, family, and God?

You and I are out here, but as the adage says, we are hard to find.

There's a serious need to revive the understanding of what manliness can do for society and how it ought to be the go-to solution for so much of what ails us. Being a man—living *manfully*—is more than outward appearances or a hardy desire for the machismo attractions—namely sex and sports—that our culture promotes. And it's certainly more than holding down a job or giving a marriage the ol' college try.

Being a man means bringing to bear the power of masculine virtue on ourselves first, our families and friends second, and society as we are able.

HOW A MAN FEELS

Give me beauty in the inward soul; may the outward and the inward man be at one.

SOCRATES, GREEK PHILOSOPHER

With manliness, more is caught than taught. Essentially, character traits and habits are often passed down to us through what we experience rather than by intentional lessons.

The way a man feels, when we're living as we should, is one of the things that should be caught at an early age. However, many of us didn't have the opportunity to catch manly virtues in our youth due to a fatherless childhood. As a result, we wonder how to find harmony between our inward self and outward self.

What a man does—his outward self—drives peace for his inner self. However, it is our soul or heart that we are looking to tend. This is where our fire lies.

When we're living our lives as we ought, we're tending to our inner world. This often appears as complementary contrasts in character. We feel confident, yet curious; ambitious, yet grateful; humble, yet capable; loving, yet sometimes violently protective.

Whereas the unsettled man feels pulled between the extremes of these character traits, the harmonious man brings his presence into them and feels his God-given authority within himself. He acts as he feels called to act, and he brings his mind and his heart to bear upon a world in which he is sorely needed. In other words, he's not afraid to show up at the show-up place—be it home or work or marriage or the gym.

There is a breadth and hardihood to a man's spirit that most men have neither seen nor felt. Let's explore a few of the areas that make up our manful selves and describe, rather idealistically, the ways in which a man ought to feel like a man.

Clarity of Mind

While clarity of mind includes clarity of purpose, I want to start by addressing it more practically. Good health has a lot to do with how well we're able to think. Having a clear mind begins with the elimination of brain fog and dullness of the mind.

In order to think clearly, we need to address our health first. Stimulants, such as coffee—of which I am a fan—can be a nice boost in the right proportions. However, too much caffeine will increase the busyness of the mind and may increase a tendency to be anxious. On the flip side, too much caffeine can actually cause sluggishness of thought as well, due to cortisol being flooded into our system to counteract the stimulant.

Water is also a critical component of a quick and lively mind. Because water is so readily available, we often take it for granted. We don't seek it out until we are well into a state of dehydration. Drinking sixteen ounces of water when you first wake up is a great way to give your mind the right start to the day.

There are many other dietary factors that affect how well our minds work. The goal here isn't to list them all but to start you down the path of optimizing your mental quickness and clarity.

Mental Clutter

Our minds are cluttered when we're preoccupied with a list of to-dos and unprocessed thoughts. The problem with mental clutter is that it distracts us from being present in the moment. As a result, we miss out on life and we're less effective.

A man whose mind is cluttered feels like he can't keep up with the pace of life. The good news is, reducing mental clutter is pretty straightforward. It requires the discipline to simply journal and plan. That's it.

Journaling helps us process the previous day and get our thoughts out of our heads and on paper. Writing is still the best way to go about this, but even if you narrate it, set aside time each day to jot down your thoughts and feelings from the day as well as any worries about the future.

Planning is another critical step to organizing your mind. Spend some time planning your week and then write down a list of things that you need to accomplish every day. Once again, this takes the clutter of the mind and organizes it by making it concrete. It reduces mental clutter and gives you more bandwidth to be present. When you're present, you'll have the feeling of actually experiencing your life.

Mental Distractions

During a normal day we're inundated by a great deal of nonsense. The really nasty thing about it is that our brains begin to orient themselves to think small. Bigger thoughts, better thoughts, and deeper thoughts become harder and are therefore avoided.

The thoughts that lead to higher ideals and clarity of purpose are traded in for those that simply gratify our longing for more nonsense: a click, a swipe, a like, a quick video. None of that really adds value to our lives.

Men, to be effective we must be vigilant about guarding our time and our minds from nonsense. There's nothing wrong with taking a break now and then, but a mind that craves constant distraction cannot be at peace nor can it ever experience clarity. Once again, the solution here is pretty simple, though it takes resolve. Take sabbaticals from social media. Suspend your accounts for a few months and stock up on books. Get away from the everyday hustle and bustle and experience the quiet of the out of doors. The sounds of nature are far more satisfying than the buzzing or chiming of a phone. Use this time as a reset for your mind. When you come back into the world of technology, you'll be aware of just how invasive it is.

When you and I feel an openness of mind and clarity of thought, we'll perform at our best. With our guiding principles closer at hand, we'll have a stronger sense of being present, intentional, and engaged in life.

Fullness of Heart

Vim, vigor, and vitality—they're three words we rarely use today, but they adequately describe the sensation we have when we feel alive. It's a feeling of our spirit being alive and well—full of gratitude and hope.

Too many of us have shrunk our hearts to match the reality in which we live, rather than the reality we wish to create. This has happened unintentionally for most of us, and it's something of an adaptation for survival. In a world of broken promises, broken trusts, failed relationships, failures of parenting, rules of conformity, miscommunication, and personal failures and shame, it's easy to see why we might shrink our hearts and fortify ourselves against a disappointing and dangerous world.

Wounds of the heart are the hardest to heal.

Unfortunately, while shrinking our hearts to protect ourselves instinctively makes sense, it actually increases the likelihood of injury. Like a small heart, a small fortress, however well protected, is still small, and any attack against it is felt by all. Even perceived threats are avoided. If we're constantly protecting ourselves from wounds of the heart, we'll keep relationships at arm's length, we won't express our expectations, and life will flow around us instead of with us and through us. The man who protects his heart can make an impact in the world, but he never allows himself to be impacted because his guard is up.

On the contrary, a man who experiences the fullness of his heart is ever-widening the territory of his heart. This expansion of our hearts allows room to experience a range of emotions while also having the bandwidth to join others in their emotions. This process—which I call a biggening of the heart—often reminds me of the Grinch. He allowed himself to feel and then to heal, which in turn grew his heart "three sizes that day." We men are not too different.

If you feel that your heart has shrunk over the years, I encourage you to find moments to experience joy and gratitude, as well as loss and sadness. As we move further into the caverns of our souls, we will become familiar with the passageways and to where they lead. We should not be afraid of any of them.

Awareness of Strength

As men, we ought to have an awareness of our physical strength. We ought to know what it is to be worked hard, to feel capable, and, on occasion, to peek over the edge of our perceived physical limitations. Far too many of us have bought into the lie that everything is downhill after forty, not realizing that we may hit our prime well into our fifties.

An awareness of strength is felt head to toe. Our muscles are engaged and our frame is steady and prepared for action. A healthy physical awareness greatly increases our feeling of confidence in ourselves and in turn increases other's confidence in us. It also puts us into a frame of mind that we're an ever-ready solution for all kinds of problems: carrying heavy things, defending the weak, intimidating your daughter's new boyfriend with a firm handshake, opening jars and certain stubborn bags of chips, breaking a seized lug nut for a tire change, throwing your daughter's *ex-boyfriend* to the curb, splitting firewood, or pushing a stalled car to safety.

Being aware of our strength has more to do with felt strength than it does with hitting a certain amount on our deadlift. It's an understanding that strength is available to be given whenever the need arises.

WHAT A MAN DOES

Health is a divine gift, and the care of the body is a sacred duty, to neglect which is to sin.

EUGEN SANDOW, STRONGMAN AND FATHER OF BODYBUILDING

A man must do manly things. We must engage our mind, body, and spirit in the daily and weekly activities that, if neglected, will leave us dull-witted, slothful, and cynical. It's key to not only do manly things, but to also do them with the mind of a man.

When engaging in manly activities, we should know that we're feeding an essential part of who God made us to be. This requires presence of mind and an intentionality in our work, our relationships, and our hobbies. Being aware that your actions lead to an overall sense of peace—inwardly and outwardly—is vital to owning your routine and having a sense of stewardship over yourself. This stewardship of ourselves serves to increase our sense of winning in life, which has a direct correlation to testosterone production.

When we're living with intentionality and purpose—taking note of the ways in which we add value in this world—testosterone levels will rise. Naturally, we will want to continue in that direction. When we're not living with intentionality, testosterone levels fall. To get our engines revved back up again, we'll have to reorient ourselves to get back on the right track.

A Man Works

A man needs meaningful, challenging work. Work affects our sense of fulfillment. There's no utopian version of manhood in which men do not put forth great effort to achieve something worthwhile. There's no retirement in manhood. The work may change through the years, but whether we're putting our hand to the plow or the keyboard—or both—work and a sense of manhood are inextricably linked.

Fulfillment in work comes through knowing we're playing a vital role in something greater than ourselves. There are a lot of things we can do that keep us mentally entertained, but the sense of fulfillment we long for happens when we realize our gifts and effort are both needed and useful in forwarding a mission that aligns with our values.

Our family—especially if we have children—is often the first instinctive sense of this mission and fulfillment paradigm that we experience.

Unfortunately, our jobs are often disconnected from the direct support of the family mission. We get a job to pay the bills to support the family, but in doing so we focus our energy and time on the mission of the business and often lose focus on our family. This is why it's key to do work that allows us to keep our family as the main thing.

It's important to make sure your employer has a mission that resonates with you. When you can feel yourself as an integral part of something larger than yourself, you will experience a sense of fulfillment in your work.

A Man Wins

Men, at our very core we are problem solvers. We're created to put the world in order. When a woman asks us to just listen instead of proposing solutions, it's kind of like asking a dog not to chase squirrels. We can do it—and we can be happy that it makes someone we love happy—but it goes against our nature.

For a man, identifying issues and righting them with ingenuity and pluck produces one of the greatest sensations we know: winning.

When we win—even in small ways—and especially when we pause to acknowledge that win, we get a spike in testosterone which in turn leads to an increase in dopamine. In short, when we win, we feel more like a man, and the dopamine tells us that feeling like a man is a reward for doing good.

A healthy counting of wins looks more like gratitude than it does chest pounding. It's important to keep a loose tether between our self-estimation and performance. Otherwise, we find ourselves seeking wins at any cost and becoming ego-driven rather than values-driven. However, taking time to pause, to recognize the good we're doing, to be thankful for where we've come from, what we've been through, and the difference that we're making is essential to a healthy sense of manly pride. While we often find it easy to speak well of the achievements of others, we find it hard to acknowledge that in ourselves. This isn't humility, it's an underdeveloped sense of dignity, and it's an epidemic among men.

While there are wins that are happening around us that simply need to be recognized, the best wins come through challenges. Some challenges are forced upon us, but others we can take up willingly. Whether it's a physical challenge or a relational challenge, step into it with the intent of breaking through barriers and coming through it a better man.

A Man is Active

We're made to be active for a great deal of the day and to operate off of a limited amount of food. For generations now, we've grown accustomed to large meals and limited movement throughout the day. Our bodies, however, are made for just the opposite. Because we've flipped the script on our natural design, weight gain and diseases of all kinds are rampant. If our day job doesn't require much from us physically, we have to enact an exercise regimen to not only stay fit but also to keep our mind sharp and fight back against depression and anxiety.

Strength training and cardio are non-negotiables when it comes to growth as a man. In fact, it's the first step to beginning the journey to manliness in earnest. Keep it simple. As long as we're training to lift, push, pull, and run in the most practical ways possible, we're on the right path.

A Man Plays

We need to get back the lost art of play. We spend too much time making goals and adding to our to-do lists, which simply feels like more work. Every man needs time where he regularly experiences joy without strings attached. Of course, we must do this with the maturity of a man. Hobbies are great, but if they detract from our character or make us worse for wear, they're not worthy of the man we want to become. Hunting, sports, shooting, card games, photography, and exercise are all great ways of having fun that don't pull us away from the path of the man we long to be.

As I'm writing this, I've realized that many of my pastimes have become businesses, so I've taken up a few new ones. In the last few years I've really become engaged in photography. I've also started to learn how to skateboard. Strangely enough, I had a few dreams about skateboarding, and in the dream I was pretty amazing at it. In reality that hasn't been the case, though I'm progressing more quickly than I expected. I've also taken up metal detecting. Old stuff fascinates me, and I love spending hours in nature looking for hidden treasures.

Worthwhile hobbies are just as important as work to the spirit of a man. While our work feeds our sense of purpose and fulfillment, our hobbies keep our spirit young and our minds fresh. Good hobbies oftentimes intersect with and add value to the work that we do in ways we couldn't have foreseen.

SO GO THE MEN, SO GO THE PEOPLE

I often find myself looking back on the lives of historical men and thinking, *Well, of course they lived more manfully. They had to.*

In some respects, I suppose that's true. The farther back we go the harder things were. Therefore, the tougher men had to be to survive and thrive. At the same time, however, there were scores of men who were quite unmanly despite living in precarious times. It makes me take a look at my own time and realize I have a choice: to be a man or to simply be.

Society tells me that either is acceptable, though the latter is preferred. However, reason, instinct, and my spirit tell me that only one is right. Have we yet plumbed the depths of the masculine waters? Has history so exhausted herself of virtuous men during the epochs of struggles towards the modern age that none are left to be fathers, husbands, and warriors?

Or, have we traded the still, deep waters for the cool, babbling brooks? Have we heeded the whisper of soft living instead of the High Call of manliness?

If you grew up without a father figure or other men to show you an example of how a man ought to live, your cave may be pretty dark. Manliness is both daunting and inviting. Fear keeps us in place even when our spirit hears the call. The bad news is, it can be hard work and the guides are few.

The good news is, as we venture farther in and begin finding that truest of timbers—manliness—our fire will burn brighter and illuminate the path ahead. Somewhere in those deep woods, another man is seeing your light blaze heavenward. You have what it takes to become not only a better man for yourself, but an inspirational man for others.

Part 2

THE 5 PRINCIPLES OF LIVING MANFULLY

3

LIVING DELIBERATELY

I went to the woods because I wished to live deliberately, to front only the essential facts of life, and see if I could not learn what it had to teach, and not, when I came to die, discover that I had not lived. I did not wish to live what was not life, living is so dear; nor did I wish to practise resignation, unless it was quite necessary. I wanted to live deep and suck out all the marrow of life, to live so sturdily and Spartan-like as to put to rout all that was not life, to cut a broad swath and shave close, to drive life into a corner, and reduce it to its lowest terms.

WALDEN; OR, LIFE IN THE WOODS,
HENRY DAVID THOREAU,
AMERICAN POET, AUTHOR, AND PHILOSOPHER

How interesting it is to read Thoreau's quote above and realize he wrote it in the mid-1800s. Typically, when we think back to that time it seems so distant as to be considered ancient. While many people were beginning to migrate into the cities, rural life was still the norm for most. A life of hard work and toil—living season to season by the sweat of one's brow—could readily be seen on the worn faces of men and women, grown old before their time.

Yet, Thoreau found that he needed to get away *to the woods* to truly confront life. Even in that early age of domesticity, the encroachment of concrete and glass was beginning to wall off man from the organic and living dust from whence he came. If Thoreau felt it then, we can certainly be justified in feeling it now.

Notice, however, the reason he went to the woods in the first place: *to live deliberately*. What does he mean by that? Does he mean that his life as a writer was not deliberate? Or that city living is somehow less deliberate than roughing it in the woods?

I would venture to guess that many people deliberately moved to the city for a number of good reasons: better working conditions, closer community, and better pay just to name a few.

I believe, for Thoreau, his idea of deliberate living was to feel the weight of true autonomy and reliance upon himself with and against the wild, which is hard to find in a settled place with a settled people. For him, comfort and ease that had not been earned were a hindrance to life and thought. As he says in his own words: "*Most of the luxuries and many of the so-called comforts of life are not only not indispensable, but positive hindrances to the elevation of mankind.*"

He could only be clearheaded enough to think through the problems which were seeming to stain the conscience of man when he was removed from a society resolved to progress. After all, a wanderer who is lost will backtrack till he finds the error along his journey. Unfortunately, Thoreau's ardent love of nature and his gift of deep introspection led him towards following his own intuition—or perhaps we should say, feelings—rather than reason, becoming a Transcendentalist—never go full Transcendentalist! Thankfully, his philosophical positions are not the subject of this chapter. I believe we can glean some insight into what it means to live deliberately, as a man, using Thoreau's flight into the wild as a jumping-off point towards a broader principle.

WORK WORTH DOING

Here is the manliness of manhood, that a man has a good reason for what he does, and has a will in doing it.

ALEXANDER MACLAREN, ENGLISH NONCONFORMIST MINISTER

Virtues and character—as important as they are—only provide a means of keeping us on the straight and narrow. They do not fulfill us. Simply being a good, virtuous man does not fill the deep well of our hearts. In fact, it makes life all the more difficult to bear.

Like Thoreau, many of us yearn for the wild. We want to jump headfirst into a life of farming, or the military, or quit our desk jobs and move to Alaska and make wooden stools. We even long for chaos. What man doesn't dream of an apocalyptic reset to the modern life in which we find ourselves? Zombies, terrorists, financial and social disasters, aliens, whatever—just bring it so we don't have to pay taxes!

I'm having fun here, but I'm not downplaying these desires. We need to keep them alive and well, and I don't think that will be an issue. A domesticated dog still loves a fight. I believe, however, that when we boil these desires down, it comes down to wanting to live a fulfilling life. The virtuous man wants a life of mission and of value. We desire to *live deliberately.*

So then, what keeps us from living as we feel we ought? I believe it's partly due to the unmanly mantras we've adopted that undermine our true desire to live a manful life. At the end of the day, fear is at the core of unintentional living.

We are Resistant to Change

Living deliberately means we need to change some aspects of how we do life. This includes how we go about growing and changing our character, but it may also include our job or family dynamics. In either case, it can only happen if we're open to change and pursuant of change. Here are a few mantras our itching ears love to believe when it suits our strong desire for complacency and apathy:

- You can't change who you are
- Just be yourself
- You are perfect just the way you are
- There is no one else like you
- This is just the way I am

I have met countless men and women who have absolutely settled in life. They look in the mirror, for example, and see a fat person who hates to exercise and say to themselves, *"I am not a runner. I am just not made for running."* So then, what are they made for? Twinkies? A couch? Thankfully, a number of these people have eventually said to themselves, *"I hate being fat. I am not a runner, but I will become one."* And they did. In fact, this happened to me.

I, Marshmallow Man

A few years after my time in the military, I saw a picture of myself in a sweater and was shocked at how fat I had become. I had jumped from about 165 pounds to 230! As a guy who is just under six feet tall, I was hauling some serious heft around and traveling down a bad road very quickly.

The picture was a wake-up call, and I committed to losing the weight. Over the next few months I cut back on buffets and sweets, and I started exercising again. One day, when I was feeling good about my progress, I decided to take off my shirt and go for a run around the track at the local YMCA. As I rounded a turn, I saw kids on a nearby playground looking my way, pointing, and then hiding as kids do. On my second lap, however, they were ready. As I got closer I could hear jeers from their wooden fortress of swings and slides. They pointed and laughed and one called out, *"Ewww, look! It's the marshmallow man!"*

I was too winded to run the little rug rats down, plus, I couldn't see through my tears. Just kidding! It was hilarious, and I was glad to see fat shaming was alive and well in the next generation. The thing is, those little brats were right. I was fat and my torso hadn't seen the sun in ages. Funny as it may have been, the truth is that I still had a long way to go. I wasn't a runner yet. In fact, I hated running. I was just a guy who had started to lose some weight, and I was feeling good about an achievement.

I needed to become a different man if my weight loss was going to stick. I needed to become someone who didn't just avoid buffets for the sake of a self-imposed diet. I needed to become someone who didn't eat at buffets because I was better than that. I didn't want to be the guy who ran around the track to burn calories so he could look better in a sweater. I wanted to be the guy who loved running for the sake of running. I had experienced some of that change when I was in boot camp, so I knew it was possible. But I needed to be a man who could motivate himself, for the sake of himself. That's a change which isn't measured in pounds, but in time.

The unhealthy mantra that we can't change who we are creates a mindset that subtly undermines our efforts to become a better man. Those mantras inspire the notion of "I wish" instead of "I will." They lead us to say, "If only" instead of "In time."

The point is, we must learn to be deliberate about our mindset if we ever hope to change.

p.s., I love to run now, but I still look terrible in a sweater.

Placing the Onus on Modern Circumstances

Blaming circumstances is an area I've struggled with quite a bit. Judging by my conversations with other men, blaming circumstances is a source of entanglement for most of us. We have a love-hate relationship with modern society. Though we have comforts that our forefathers could have only dreamed of, we have an unrequited desire for wildness that we carry as both a burden and a badge of manhood.

In this passion for wildness, we place our hopes in living as a man ought to live—at least how we think he ought to live. In the woods, axe in hand, rifle at the ready, straight-shooting sons, hard-working, grit-filled daughters, and a wife kept lean and beautiful by the dirt in the field and laughter with her family. And we think we could have that life too if it weren't for the damned gub'ment! *Wake up sheeple! One day, it will all come crashing down and we'll be ready, just you wait!*

Or perhaps your circumstances are the simple, soul-sucking drudgery of your J.O.B. You didn't ask for this life, right? Blue-collar? White-collar? *How about no collar? Collars are for dogs, not wolves!*

Blaming our circumstances sounds like this: *If only people would just (fill in the blank). If only society would just (fill in the blank). Then I could live as a man!*

It's ironic that manliness comes through adversity, and yet adversity is the thing we so often want to solve. A man who can't find some admirable duty to perform in a time of peace and prosperity is merely a soldier. The man who can, well, that man is a king.

The Disgusting Premise of Retirement

There was a time in the history of America when people worked themselves nearly to death. I say nearly because they didn't always work themselves completely to death, but they worked themselves to the point of no longer being able to work. Thus, they would retire.

At some point, people began not working themselves nearly enough to death, so the age of retirement at sixty-five meant twenty more years of living. If you saved up enough funds and the markets treated you squarely, you could then live like a king for those remaining years. The problem is that too many men are waiting for that day to come with an unnatural and unmanly eagerness. The idea of retirement is no longer just financial security in old age. It has been marketed as a second life. It's the life you were meant to live when you were young but never did due to the demands of a career which would provide for your retirement.

The disgusting premise of retirement is this: One day, when the kids are out of the house, the house is paid for, and your bank account is full, then you can live. Or even worse, then you can take it easy. Until then, you work.

There's nothing wrong with saving money and taking full advantage of the tax benefits available. However, when it comes down to putting $2,500 away in the IRA versus taking the family to Yosemite, Disney, or on a mission trip, I say do the latter. Don't let retirement be a time of regretting a wasted youth. Pour your life into your family and others, then work at doing some good until you breathe your last.

A Good Reason for What He Does

In the Alexander Maclaren quote that opened this section, he says the manliness of manhood—which I believe is the essence of what we deem manly—is that he "has a good reason for what he does." I think the word *good* in this quote can be easily overlooked. Perhaps we think it to mean convincing or reasonable, but I think he means good in the truest sense of the word: as in good versus evil. We have a number of reasonable things that we do, but we lack fulfillment because very few of them are actually good.

When a man spends his day doing things that don't align with his values, there's a space left in his soul. There's a chasm which must be crossed, for on the other side is his purpose and his calling. The challenge of our time is that we've been told that this unsatisfied and unclear longing is due to a lack of personal happiness. And so we move through jobs, marriages, homes, and cars with a me-focused way of living. Some men have resorted to alcohol and drugs for pleasure and escape, while others have tried to continue their boyhood indefinitely in an effort to hold on to that feeling of excitement that comes from the lack of responsibilities and routine.

Our inability to judge good work from merely reasonable work is deeply connected to our most basic understanding of how this world operates—what we call our worldview. We can't rightly answer the question *What will satisfy my manly heart?* because so many of us are still asking the question *What is the good, the truest good in this world, that a man ought to be about?*

Men, this question should have been answered for us long ago. Until we're convinced of the answer, we'll be at odds with the very laws of nature and of nature's God.

Failing to Launch

The failure of young people in America to launch into adulthood is an ironic predicament. At a time when we have more opportunity for employment in every field of study—a time when people of nearly every social class can obtain a world-class education—young adults are going through college, going into debt, and moving back in with their parents. These children have been dubbed "Boomerang Kids."

But the problem of failing to launch is much broader than post-college inertia. Men are apathetic in their careers. They're not committing to marriage. They're not fathering their children. And they're not active in their communities and government. Younger generations of men are living listless and apathetic lives in increasing numbers. And while many would see this failure to launch as merely a lack of motivation and laziness, I believe it's actually rooted in fear. Let me explain.

The Questions We Were Not Allowed to Ask

There are questions a boy ought to be encouraged to ask and be given an earnest answer: "*Why am I here? What is this life all about? What good am I to do?*"

Yet in recent generations, kids haven't been encouraged to ask these questions. And if they do, parents don't know how to respond. They don't want to point them too strongly towards religion, because they don't have firm religious beliefs themselves. They're worried it will make an everlasting impression upon the naïve minds of their kids and lead to irrational thought, a serious disregard for science, and an increase in wars, judgmentalism, and televangelists. So instead they say, "*Some people believe that we were created by God, and he is in control of everything.*" Or "*Some people believe that we're all here as part of a cosmic accident.*"

Of course, this leads the child to ask, *"Daddy, what do you believe?"* And what should our response be? For this is the very question, that if we had an answer we truly believed in, we would know our own purpose and have our good reason for what we do. Alas, when we were at that tender age and asked these questions—when our minds and hearts were full of wonder and expectations of the great good of this world—the answer was typically either an unconvincing belief in God or an equally unconvincing belief that our ancestors were apes.

Though evolution teaches that it has been millions of years since our ancestors were apes, in the child's textbook it's only two or three pages prior that our ancestors were the muck on the rocks. And so, we go through the years of boyhood unconvinced and unsatisfied, and enter into adulthood numbed to the great question, and yet we live with an unrelenting ache from our desire to ask it.

All the while, we're told to find fleeting glimmers of joy and happiness along the way: girlfriends, money, music, sports, drugs, and anything that entertains. Our happiness in life seems to be bound together with our ability to make good decisions. So, we arrive at the foothills of life in our twenties with the pressure to set off over the range towards happiness.

We firmly believe our success in life is dependent upon our ability to make the right choices. Marry the right girl. Settle in the right town. Choose the right career. The consequences of making the wrong decision can wreck our life. We've been told that if we "love what we do we'll never work a day in our life." That sounds really nice, but what if we don't know what we love to do? Or what if we grow bored with it? What if—and this is the big one—we do our best and find out we don't have what it takes? What if we find out that we're not good enough at life to ensure our happiness? Then what?

Further complicating the situation, the larger decisions we are required to make often mean sacrificing current pleasures without knowing when we can enjoy them again. We are bound by fear. We are intimidated by the realization of our lack of manhood and the weight of the decisions before us. So, we stay close to home, camping in familiar territory rather than venturing, fearless, into a world of grand possibility.

It is here that our fires need to be tended. We need that steady burn which thaws our fear. In that dark cave lies the answers to the questions of our boyhood: *Why am I here? What good am I to do?* And though we never knew it, the answers are the great timbers of our life—the weight of which only a man can heave.

I don't believe those questions are created by us. I don't believe the answers are all that different from man to man. I believe these questions were placed in our conscience by the One who created it. The Eternal One who creates each man and sets his fire before him. It stands to reason, then, that if we didn't create the questions, we can't create the answer. I believe that—though the same answer untethers that hearty stock for our use—each man must put his own back into the work of ensuring its good use, living out his life as he wills, and tending to his own fire with holy reverence. I believe the answer is thus:

> "He has told you, O man, what is good; and what does the Lord require of you but to do justice, and to love kindness, and to walk humbly with your God?"—Micah 6:8, The Bible, ESV

> "The end of the matter; all has been heard. Fear God and keep his commandments, for this is the whole duty of man."—Ecclesiastes 12:13, The Bible, ESV

> "And you shall love the Lord your God with all your heart and with all your soul and with all your mind and with all your strength. The second is this: You shall love your neighbor as yourself. There is no other commandment greater than these."—Mark 12:30-31, The Bible, ESV

Men, the truth is, our good work should have started in our boyhood, not when we got out of high school or college. Other men should have helped us tend to our fire. We should have been taught to answer those questions as well as the hard, rewarding, and manly work of living a life out of a belief in the High Calling of manliness.

As fathers, uncles, and mentors this is now our calling and our responsibility. Rather than living for the sake of personal happiness and the pressure that comes along with it, we live our lives in honor of God, pursuing the good of others, and loving with all of the strength our manly heart can bear. This is the good work we long for. That is living deliberately.

LEARNING TO LOVE HARD WORK

The man who learns to love hard work will love all of life.

JOHN STOTT, CRAFTSMEN

I first read the quote above in John Stott's book *Craftsmen*. That simple phrase has stuck with me more than anything else in that excellent little work. I have often recited it on my website, Wolf & Iron, and said it to my own boys. I'm hoping that over time the truth of this quote will sink in and adjoin their budding manliness.

I've also said it for my own benefit, as it's something I need to be reminded of quite often. When I was the age of my sons—who are thirteen and sixteen as I write this—the idea of loving hard work would have seemed absurd. My youngest is a great reflection of me in this way. When I tell him that *"you can learn to love hard work,"* he says, *"Why would anyone want to do that? If there is an easy way to do something, then why would you want to do something hard?"*

Herein lies the difference between boyhood and manhood. A man is aware that he craves not ease but sweat. He knows that what ultimately satisfies him is what challenges him. He longs to be spent out for some noble deed.

PURSUIT OF ALL THAT IS NOT EASY

There has never yet been a man in our history who led a life of ease whose name is worth remembering.

THEODORE ROOSEVELT, 26TH PRESIDENT OF THE UNITED STATES, ROUGH RIDER, AND MAN

Between the ages of nine and thirteen I lived with my grandparents in the country. I loved mowing the acres of land on a riding lawn mower, swinging by one of the apple trees in the orchard, and picking an apple right off the branch. They were Golden Delicious, but they were hardier, smaller, and tougher than the apples you typically find in stores. The good ones had golden flecks on them. I loved to throw the core in front of the mower and watch the pieces fly. This was not hard work.

The work I hated came on Saturday mornings. Since we didn't have cable TV in the country and this was before the age of the internet, Saturday mornings were the only time to watch cartoons. For my younger readers, I'm sure this sounds terrible. We actually had to schedule our life around the television timetable rather than watching what we wanted whenever we wanted.

Unfortunately, my granddaddy didn't watch cartoons and had already been up since the crack of dawn trimming branches on the apple, plum, and peach trees. Just when I was about to settle into watching an episode of He-Man or G.I. Joe, he would come into the house and tell me I had some work to do. Not only had I been waiting for my cartoons all week, but I had been playing with He-Man and G.I. Joe toys as well in anticipation for this event—which I believed was my reason for living.

Saturday mornings often meant taking care of mountains of branches or a truck bed full of scrap wood from granddaddy's construction business. He would back the truck up to the edge of the old Hatchie River, and I would spend what felt like hours tossing every scrap into a burn pile. I suppose it would make a great story if all of the throwing had trained my arm to be an excellent pitcher or a quarterback, but alas that didn't happen. For me, this was hard work, and I hated it.

However, after a few years of this, something began to change. I found myself enjoying certain types of difficult chores. We heated the house with wood, so my granddaddy would regularly fell some tree. He would get a load of wood up from the Hatchie River bottom and onto our property. Before too long I was splitting and stacking that wood all by myself. Henry Ford was right when he said, "Chop your own wood and it will warm you twice." This was hard work, but I didn't hate it. In fact, I loved it. I loved the time alone splitting wood and tending to the stack. My thoughts coming and going without interruption, and finally seeing that wood come into the house by the armful to warm the family. This was good work. In this transaction—from field to the flame—I could see the whole purpose of my hard work, just as my granddaddy could see it in the pruning and care of the orchard.

Sometimes the hard work that we ought to love is physical, but oftentimes it's mental or emotional. It's hard work to tend to a marriage that isn't working. It's hard work to build up character in a resistant child. It's hard work to admit when we're wrong. It's hard work to bridle our tongue or speak a good word in due season. It's hard work to get off our duffs and exercise.

I have, on a number of occasions, had to confront a pastor about some things I felt were wrong. In every one of those instances, I was the younger of the two of us, and it took boldness to say what I believe needed to be said. That was hard work, and it didn't always result in a resolution. I've had that same experience as a father, husband, and friend.

Though it's a different kind of hard work, I still think back to my granddaddy coming into the house and interrupting my Saturday morning cartoons. That feeling of hard work needing to be done—with both dread and fear of what I may lose in the process—is often replaced with gratitude in the remembrance of what I gained.

The hard work of life is like going into the recesses of that deep cavern. The light of our convictions illuminates the path ahead, and the stronger our fire the more clearly we can see. Daunting though the way ahead may be, a man moves forward knowing that where our strength is tested, our strength is made full, and that the hard work which needs to be done is the work of a man.

THE HIGH CALL OF MANLINESS

Far and away the best prize that life has to offer is the chance to work hard at work worth doing.

THEODORE ROOSEVELT, 26TH PRESIDENT OF THE UNITED STATES, HUNTER, THIEF WRANGLER, AND MAN

There is a High Calling in being a man. We feel it in the way danger beckons us, makes us weak in the knees, unsure of ourselves, and yet swells our hearts to action. And like the Siren call to Odysseus, we know the only way forward is through. We hear the call of manliness in the suffering of the weak, and soon find that the suffering of the afflicted, and our risk, are bound together in the honor and duty of manhood.

The High Call of manliness appeals to our noblest senses. It bids us to come forward and to take up the work. It calls us to discover what's good and true in the world and to bring our manliness to bear upon it.

If we lack courage to answer the call, may we find it. If we lack ability, may we lean upon one another. If we lack faith, may God grant it to us.

4

LIVING COURAGEOUSLY

Faced with what is right,
to leave it undone shows lack of courage.

CONFUCIUS, CHINESE PHILOSOPHER, POLITICIAN, AND TEACHER

Within each man resounds the desire for a singular act of valor. We each have a desire to experience the pride swell of usefulness and bold courage. We long to be cast in the role of hero at least once in our own story.

To say this desire is only the result of Hollywood's undoubted influence on men to be the proverbial John McClane in the Nakatomi Plaza of their life, is to dismiss the ages of men and their stories of heroism. For some men, a daring act in the face of sacrifice may arrive unannounced and unwelcomed. Yet for many of us, a significant act of bravery will remain in the realm of daydreams, virtual affrays, and theatre seating. What a welcomed and disappointing reality! It embodies the result of the ordered and peaceful existence so long hoped for, and the loss of the heroism that was necessary to obtain it. As men, we still desire a good battle and a noble engagement.

A man's mind is hardwired to appreciate a singular event rather than the long and patient pursuit of a goal. We hail the summit rather than the climb. We wrongly assume that displays of courage come as leaps rather than countless unwavering steps. By doing so, we miss the commonplace opportunities to act courageously. Thus, we can wait our whole lives for the opportunities that were all around us. Then when the time comes where a leap of heroism is needed, we find ourselves woefully inadequate. Let it not be so for us.

THE COURAGE TO BE COURAGEOUS

There is an often overlooked first step in becoming a man of courage: a willingness to be *that guy*. This is more than mere admiration of courage or fantasies of glory. It is prior to the will to act. It is seeing oneself as having a responsibility to do what is right and a resolute acceptance of failure if it comes. This is not a hope for failure, of course, but an understanding that action which requires courage often includes the risk of sacrifice.

The man who is not willing to fail is not willing to act. To be *that guy* also means to possess the initial courage to hold one's self to a standard—to seek the high ground—and to possibly face the ridicule of those who remain in the valleys. When we're in the presence of a man of principles it causes us to reflect upon ourselves, and, in comparison, feel the contrast of character and want of grit.

I would be wrong to say that this *First Courage* comes only from reflection and resolution. First Courage often comes from the pluck of a nonconformist. The impulse to think for himself may serve a man well, provided he is guided and rooted in truth. Where First Courage stems from is less important than the need for a man to have it. We may call it pluck, daring, boldness, or stubbornness, yet a man cannot truly know that he has it until the time comes when he is tested. Then his courage either stands firm or blows over.

It's only upon reflection that he sees his unwavering will preceding the event that prepared him for the test. After passing the test, he truly knows himself to be a man of courage. Passion is not enough to know we have First Courage. Knowledge of what is right will not make us courageous. Good character in easy times will not reveal courage. We can only know our courage in the moment—or many moments—of either action or inaction.

Developing First Courage

Some people think First Courage is something a man either has or doesn't have. To say that some men are not outfitted with the gift of courage at the factory would be amiss. In some boys we observe boldness and courage at an early age that follows them into manhood. Yet to say that courage cannot be put on aftermarket would also be incorrect. The nature of a man is pliable. Just as good men can become cruel when given authority over others, a timid man can become a man of daring.

My friend, some iron must go into the fire longer before it can be worked to good use. Honor the iron you are.

The truth is, First Courage exists within each of us, though it's weaker in some than in others. Developing initial courage is like working a weak muscle. For the timid, developing courage means purposefully exercising that which is weak to make it strong.

A Brotherhood of Courage

Accountability with other men is the first leap we can take over the chasm of cowardice to courage. With accountability we not only commit to holding ourselves to a higher standard, we openly call for others to do so as well. Trusting others to hold you accountable, to handle the reins, and to crack the whip of one's life is certainly courageous.

When we're accountable to other men, we must square ourselves with the reality of our own giftings and failings. It's like walking into a gym in shorts knowing we've been skipping leg day our entire life and asking everyone to critique us! Accountability with honorable men also dares a man to heed the advice that's given him and to trust in a map that is not his own in hopes of reaching a land he has never seen: *Courage.*

High Moral Courage

Mark Twain had a way of representing the timeless characteristics of mankind like few men since. He once wrote, *"It is curious that physical courage should be so common in the world and moral courage so rare."*

This is certainly as true today as it was in his time. With physical courage, a man bounds towards danger. With moral courage, he bounds towards truth. Physical danger puts us in jeopardy of losing our well-being and possibly our lives. Moral danger puts the well-being of our souls in jeopardy.

In the most esteemed acts of courage, we often see both physical and moral courage. A man who is guided by heart, mind, and body in a selfless and sacrificial act is the highest display of courage and manhood. Yet, I believe moral courage is the greater of the two as it only exists when a man, himself, is changed. His courage is not only a physical act—daring and bold and necessary—he is also a being of true nature. By performing an act of moral courage, he has been made good within so that he may do good without.

Numerous are the men throughout history who have been celebrated for their acts of physical bravery despite their immoral causes for which they were fighting. The Nazi soldier dashed from his trench the same as every Allied troop. Pirates and bank robbers have long been the idols of many a boy. Regardless of their murdering and ribald lives, they are celebrated for their pluck, rebellion, craftiness, luck, and feats.

I mean, the balls on these guys, right!?

Then, in steps the hero of the story. He fights for truth and justice, for God and country, and for those who cannot. Marauders and thieves may escape with your imagination and your wallet, but the hero steals your heart.

Robert Shaw's "Swamp Angels"

By 1863 the American Civil War was taking its toll on the lives and fortunes of the North. In need of men to fight, the Union Army set out to form all-black regiments made up of mostly freed slaves. Though Northerners opposed slavery, they still considered blacks inferior to their white counterparts and suspected a lack of bravery and performance under fire.

So, when Captain Robert Gould Shaw was offered the post of Commanding the first all-black regiment, he declined.

Shaw was a man of undoubted courage and a stern abolitionist, but the thought of raising, training, and leading a group of black soldiers called to witness the depth of his convictions. He had fought on the fields of battle since he was a young boy, including leading soldiers in the fierce and bloody battle of Antietam. As for physical courage, he seemingly had both portion and reserve. But the Commanding of a "negro" regiment would require a moral courage of which he was unsure. The post was considered a demotion by many. The all-black unit and its commander would be continually buffeted with ridicule, possibly abandoned in the field, and left to fend for themselves.

If Shaw accepted the position and failed, it would not only be a detriment to his career, it would also be a strike against the colored man in a land where he hoped to be called not only free, but equal.

A few days after declining the post, Shaw changed his mind and accepted. On February 8th, 1863, he wrote the following in a letter to his fiancé:

> "After I have undertaken this work, I shall feel that what I have to do is to prove that a negro can be made a good soldier, and, that being established, it will not be a point of honour with me to see the war through, unless I really occupied a position of importance in the army. … You know how many eminent men consider a negro army of the greatest importance to our country at this time. If it turns out to be so, how fully repaid the pioneers in the movement will be, for what they may have to go through! And at any rate I feel convinced I shall never regret having taken this step, as far as I myself am concerned; for while I was undecided I felt ashamed of myself, as if I were cowardly."—Robert G. Shaw

Shame. It's the ghost of cowardice. It haunts the man who rejects the call to act upon the demands of his conscience. Like Shaw, we feel it in our bones when we're persuading ourselves to take a less honorable path. Resigning our moral responsibility leaves a vacancy that's filled by shame and later accompanied by contempt for ourselves and our lack of action. Shaw's decision to man up, to play the man over his fears, changed him and made history.

The 54th Massachusetts Infantry Regiment became a strong force of men—exemplary in their courage and feared as warriors. Shortly after Shaw accepted the position, the 54th and two white regiments mounted an assault against an overwhelming force in Charleston, South Carolina. In the fire of battle, Shaw ascended a parapet. With sword in hand he called a charge to his men, *"Forward, fifty-fourth, forward!"*

He was struck down in a moment of glory.

Shaw was buried in a common grave with his "negros" that fell in the battle. The grave was intended as an insult, but it could not have been a greater honor for the man.

The actions of the 54th, on that day and those to come, changed the minds of many. The black man was proven as formidable a soldier as any man. The 54th Massachusetts Infantry Regiment became the foundation for the famed Buffalo Soldiers—the nickname given to a regiment of all-black U.S. Army soldiers raised shortly after the Civil War.

Overcoming the Shame of Moral Failure

Shame is a prominent figure in the lives of many men. Though the life we desire to live is modeled by men such as Robert Shaw or heroes of our own time, many of us have a past that is far from the lives of these honorable men. Sometimes our failures are so evident that we can't see a path from the man we are to the man we wish to become.

The apparition of shame throws shade on our quest to manhood. Men who feel ashamed of their past often find themselves in a catch-22. We want redemption for our failings, but we lack the confidence to succeed. The attempted resolution of this dilemma generally comes at two extreme ends on the spectrum of action. On one end, we're reluctant to move into the path of danger where our courage will be required and tested. On the other, we are rash, throwing ourselves into any challenge to try to redeem our manhood. Both of these approaches to dealing with shame tend to deepen the wound and confirm the belief that *I don't have what it takes.*

Throwing off the weight of shame is not a matter of action. It isn't necessary to prove we're a man to cancel the debt of shame. The direct approach to overcoming shame rarely works—we must flank it.

How? A man must be willing to forgive himself for his moral failures. This comes easiest and most completely when a man knows the forgiveness of Christ. If the Maker of all things can offer forgiveness to you and me, who are we to hold a grudge against ourselves?

We often become attached to our guilt. It can be tough and soul-exhausting work for a man to let go and forgive himself. However, it can also come in an instant. Though you may trek many miles to find forgiveness, you'll soon realize it was always within reach.

Forgiveness burns bright in a man, casts all shadows behind him, warms the spirit, and lights the way forward.

DARING PHYSICAL COURAGE

A man's usefulness depends upon his living up to his ideals insofar as he can. It is hard to fail but it is worse never to have tried to succeed. All daring and courage, all iron endurance of misfortune make for a finer, nobler type of manhood.

THEODORE ROOSEVELT, 26TH PRESIDENT OF THE UNITED STATES, LT. COLONEL, AND MAN

When we think of courage we typically think of physical acts: the squeeze of a trigger, the releasing of an arrow, the taking of a bullet, or the snatching of a child from oncoming traffic. When we recognize danger, yet fail to act, it's a lack of manhood and a failing of courage when it's needed most.

While physical courage may come about without clear moral courage, true moral courage will always manifest itself in a physical act. A man must stand, or must speak, or must fight. Or a man must restrain himself against the use of action. This too is a noble mark on a man's character. In all accounts of physical action, a man wills his body to respond in the face of danger.

I Didn't Think About It, I Just Acted

When we read an account of some courageous act, we often hear our hero say, *"I didn't think about it, I just did it."* That gives the ironic impression of being a humble yet satisfactory answer: his courage is innate. In the replay of the event we have a perspective that our hero did not. We see the danger from a different perspective—the oncoming train, the woman on the tracks, or the hero throwing himself boldly in harm's way while so many others looked on in horror. The average man would be frozen with fear at the thought of what would happen if he risked his own life to save someone else, as well as the consequences of not doing so. But, this is not the case for our hero.

This has always left me wondering: Is it a heroic act of courage if the hero did not overcome fear?

Men such as Theodore Roosevelt—though they are few—are invigorated by danger. They go looking for danger. There's a famous picture that was taken of Roosevelt and his Rough Riders on a ship when they're returning to the States after taking San Juan Hill in Cuba. Most of the men look battle-worn and weary, but Roosevelt looks like a man made anew.

Once again this raises the question, is it a courageous act if the man did not wrestle with fear?

Channeling Fear into Action

To answer this question for Theodore Roosevelt, we need to understand his childhood and his life as a young man. We often find ourselves looking at the sum, but not the figures and calculations that went into it. We see the Olympians in all of their glory, but not the years of training behind them.

As a boy, Roosevelt was sickly and near death on a regular basis. As we read his memoirs, we see him in bed for a week and then out on an adventure the next. To him, it was standard fare for a body that was frail, unreliable, and seemingly treasonous to a mind and soul that wanted so badly to explore and live the wild life of boyhood. However, if we could have witnessed the spirit of a young Roosevelt lying down and rising up again, we would have celebrated his courage. So, when we read about Colonel Roosevelt returning from war aglow, we're seeing the sum total of years where courage was taken in hand, brought to its feet, and passivity was left in the dust. It is as Mark Twain says, *"Courage is resistance to fear, mastery of fear—not absence of fear."*

For Roosevelt, and many others in which we witness a similar character, the mastery of fear has been practiced so regularly that it's become habit. The will has rutted in the mind a well-traveled path to courage over fear. Circumstances and emotions that blind the fearful are the same conditions that bolster the excitement and action of the courageous.

By developing courage, you and I can do this as well.

FINDING COURAGE

Courage is not created. It is summoned.

When we need courage and find ourselves lacking, we feel as though there's a missing piece in our hearts. Maybe courage was never there. Or maybe it never matured or it was broken at some early age.

The truth is, courage is not a singular element. Like most virtues, courage is the weaving together of other virtues. It's a call to arms of united forces by way of the will. As C.S. Lewis states in *The Screwtape Letters*, *"Courage is not simply one of the virtues, but the form of every virtue at the testing point, which means at the point of highest reality."*

What does Lewis mean by the "point of highest reality"? I believe he means that a virtue is only true if it can withstand testing. Moral courage must give rise to daring physical courage, or it's no better than political posturing. The spineless can only stand for so long.

The backbone of noble courage is comprised of three essential virtues.

Paul, an apostle of Christ, gives us insight into the components of courage in his letter to Timothy, a young man and an early leader in the church. In his letter to Timothy, Paul writes, *"For God gave us a spirit not of fear, but of power and love and self-control"* (2 Timothy 1:7).

I find it interesting that Paul does not say, "For God gave us a spirit not of fear, but of *courage*." Instead, he gives us the essential elements of godly, noble courage: power, love, and self-control. And he makes it clear that these come from the Almighty as a gift in the form of spirit.

"*But Mike*," you might be thinking, "*can't a man have power, love, and self-control without being a Christian?*"

Of course he can. But apart from the Spirit of God, a man is drawing these qualities from an impure source: himself. Paul says that the Spirit of God, which is in a Christian, is devoid of fear. It is power, love, and self-control in its purest form.

Power

The power which we are seeking is not merely willpower. Effort on our part is required, certainly, but there's a difference between tapping into the finite well of our own resolve and the infinite well of the immaterial, fathomless, and spiritual which God provides.

Love

When we bring love into the equation of courage, we bring forth the most admirable attributes of humanity: love for our fellow man, love for truth, love for peace, and love for the weak. Without love being brought to bear, courage would lack its nobility and a man would not find honor in his actions.

Self-Control

Fear gives rise to a lack of self-control and impulsivity. Courage—at least the type we seek—has a resolve that's grounded in principled beliefs. Most of the courageous acts in our lives will be those born out of self-control, deliberation, and forethought. While there will be moments when there can be no hesitation to act, most of life is built upon our daily thoughts and beliefs. Our daily thoughts will determine the direction in which we move. A life walked out in positive, courageous thought will look very different from one swept along by fear.

I believe 19th-century non-conformist minister Alexander Maclaren sums this up for us quite well.

> Paul points to the proper effects of the gift of God, as the ground of his counsel That Spirit does not infuse cowardice, which blenches at danger or shrinks from duty, as probably Timothy was tempted to do; but it breathes 'power' into the weak, enabling them to do and bear all things, and 'love,' which makes eager for service to God and man, at whatever cost, and 'self-control,' which curbs the tendencies to seek easy tasks and to listen to the voices within or without whispering ignoble avoidance of the narrow way. Surely this exhortation in its most general form should come to all young hearts, and summon them to open their doors for the entrance of that Divine Helper who will make them strong, loving, and masters of themselves.

THE COURAGE AND CONFIDENCE CONNECTION

Confidence is a type of steady courage. It's a walk in the sunlight of an indwelling assurance. We'll grasp it when we've learned this universal truth: Though I may succeed or I may fail, I'm resilient enough to weather the consequences of either outcome.

You may wonder, *What are the consequences for succeeding?* Many men do not move forward towards success because they fear the weight of responsibility for future success. This happens even in the areas in which they are gifted and called. Doing something well often means being called to do it again but with new expectations of a positive outcome. Fear tells us that expectations lead to pressure, pressure leads to anxiety, and anxiety leads to the inability to perform.

A man's greatest fear is a person, thought, or circumstance which may snuff out the flame of his heart. The inability to adequately perform in an area which he feels called is to lick your fingers, reach into his heart, and pinch the wick of life within him.

Many men feel as though this threat will most likely happen when their true self is on display. That in a moment of vulnerability, he will fail. And that those within striking distance—his wife, parents, peers, and children—will, with a careless or malevolent word, blow out the most precious fire of his soul.

But you and I are stronger than that.

WHERE CONFIDENCE COMES FROM

While courage and confidence are linked, a man whose head is held upright expresses himself through two particular character traits: humility and self-compassion. These two virtues can be expressed as an outward display of courage—humility—and an inward display of courage—self-compassion.

Humility

The man who is fearful takes a defensive stance towards others. As an observer it's easy to see, but when we're overly sensitive to the opinions of others it's often difficult for us to recognize. Over the years of Wolf & Iron, I've seen prominent men—men who speak of being stolid and unmoved by the estimations of others—go on a tangent of self-defense when someone dares to disagree with them.

Humility asks us to be vulnerable and content with our position as servant or savant. Humility doesn't mean we can't defend our honor and our name, but the man who walks in humility will be more concerned with bringing his strength to bear in the aid of others than exerting energy in defense of himself.

Self-Compassion

While you have no doubt heard the terms self-confidence and self-esteem, self-compassion may be a new concept for you. It's simply saying to ourselves that *It's okay to fail.*

To esteem means to hold in high regard, and self-esteem has long been touted as the wellspring of confidence. But in our defense of the pride that keeps our esteem high, we cannot allow forces to work contrary to the internal praise which keeps us feeling elevated. We've all seen the results of a man who's unwilling to endure any admonition of character or reproval of behavior. He soon finds himself alone and left to the thoughts that keep him isolated. Bitterness and cynicism are sure to follow.

However, the man who practices self-compassion in the midst of failure has grace upon himself and trusts the nature of his heart. He finds his spirit resilient. And in each failure, he finds a lesson that he is willing to heed.

COURAGE AT THE TESTING POINT

As C.S. Lewis states, courage is "the form of every virtue at the testing point." This means that in order to find courage—in order to develop it as a defining element of your nature—other virtues need to be tested.

To bring about this change in our lives, we must summon First Courage. We must take it upon ourselves to be a man who dares when others would decamp. We must make it a regular habit to step into situations that we would have formerly avoided. We must do the things that both excite and intimidate us, for courage and confidence are found in both the rewarding of our God-given talents and passions as well as overcoming our inadequacies. When we shake off passivity and begin to live deliberately, we move in a direction that hones the iron qualities of manhood and welds together the scaffolding of the man we wish to be.

Creating Testing Points

Creating testing points for courage and confidence is not complicated. In fact, they were once a natural part of life.

In the country, during my formative years, I found that I could be useful and trusted with tasks that I had only seen given to adults. During the winter I split and stacked wood and made fires for the family. After a successful hunt, my grandmother, grandfather, and I would work together to process the meat that would later become our meals. I could identify where cuts of meat began and ended and parse them accordingly. I learned how to remove silverskin and package meat for the freezer. As I grew older, my responsibilities increased as well. I mowed a few acres of grass, picked and carried apples from our orchard to elderly neighbors, hunted alone, and worked in construction.

I learned—by way of the natural setting in which I grew up—that I could pass many testing points and do the things of which I was formerly unsure.

Men, how many of us have only known a world laid out for us? How many of us shy away when faced with the broken world that calls out to be put in order?

In our manhood, we find that we can't always make up for past failures, especially those of our parents or the culture in which we were raised, but we can make up for lost time. The lessons which we could have learned in our youth can now be understood by the adult mind.

In fact, it isn't until we become adults that many of the lessons in our youth become clear.

So, if you missed out on lessons that could have brought confidence to a young heart, please understand that you are not that far removed from the revelations that will move you toward the man you feel called to be. This is a lifelong process. Reflection and application often do not begin until well into adulthood.

The ways in which you purposefully create testing points will be uniquely yours, but here are some ideas to throw on the fire. I have taken up many of these myself.

- **Travel**—This is not something we did as a family when I was growing up. The idea of vacations and sightseeing was foreign to me, and I realized it had become an area of fear as well. Now I love to travel and plan several trips each year.

- **Get punched in the face**—There's a popular phrase among men that doesn't seem to have an originator: "Every man should get punched in the face once in his life." This is best done through boxing or sparring in martial arts instead of simply picking a fight on the street.

- **Commit to a diet**—I don't mean so that you can drop fifteen pounds and then gain twenty-five pounds back. I mean a legitimate, healthy, lifelong diet. Food has one of the tightest grips on us, and frankly, it's embarrassing. I guarantee you will learn things about yourself when you have to dig deep to find the courage to tell yourself no.

- **Date your wife**—Intimacy is a challenge for a lot of men, including me. This is an area I'm growing in, and one of the main ways to do this is to show up and do the work.

Do you have the courage to be intimate with your wife in a non-sexual way?

- **Wear what you like**—Forget the trends, do what you want. For some, this may not sound like much, but for those who have a fear of being judged, it's a big step. The ability to confidently walk into a room always begins with a willingness to be yourself.

- **Grow that mustache**—I honestly just wanted to put the word mustache somewhere in this chapter. Mission accomplished! However, a happenin' stache is a bold statement and there aren't enough in the world.

- **Share your thoughts in person**—Sharing your thoughts on social media is not the same as looking someone in the eye and telling them what you believe. Are you willing to engage on a sensitive subject? Are you willing to be challenged on your views? Confident men can handle ideas objectively and enjoy discourse with those who don't agree with them.

- **Commit to a stupid race**—A 5k, 10k, duathlon, mud run, or whatever, just sign up and do it. Yes, we live in a soft world, so we have to purposefully put difficult things in front of ourselves. Plus, you'll get a t-shirt!

This list is just a teaser—something to get the juices flowing. It's up to you to search your own heart and know where you want to show up strong in life. That's where your battle is going to be. That's where the work needs to be done.

HARDWOODS MAKE THE BEST STEEL

Before coal was discovered under the hills of the Appalachians, Americans made charcoal from hardwoods. Our untamed land was awash in aged oaks and hickory, and the land needed to be cleared for settlement. Those old trees were cut down and stacked into massive mounds, set ablaze, and then covered with dirt. The wood underneath continued to burn until only black bricks of carbon remained. The smelters of the day used this charcoal to convert iron ore into steel because it burned more evenly and produced a better result. The old steel, if you can find it, is still prized above what is produced today.

The thing about hardwoods is that they grow slowly—the slower the growth, the denser the grain. But when they come into their own, they can be harvested for all types of noble uses for which the average tree is unfit. The hardwoods are heavier and harder to work, but their hewn timbers will stand for generations.

As you feed the fire of your soul, realize that some woods are fit for kindling and others for the bitter nights. Still, others are set aside to forge the armor of warriors and the swords of kings.

The tales of battle and the heroes of war can serve to light the fire of courage in a man's heart. To forge iron that is fit for battle, a man must fell the venerable hardwoods all about him. He does so in due time and by careful selection and the work of his hands. The forest must be leveled and a clearing made, for the day will come when he creates a home for himself and those he loves.

5

LIVING VIRTUOUSLY

Life, like every other blessing, derives its value from its use alone. Not for itself, but for a nobler end the Eternal gave it; and that end is virtue.

SAMUEL JOHNSON, ENGLISH WRITER, ESSAYIST, AND MORALIST

A man ought to be an observer of his own time and age; to see himself passing through his years as so many others have through theirs, to take heed of the small markers along the course of his life, and to charge himself with this question: *Am I becoming a man of merit?*

Some may ask, *Am I becoming a man I can be proud of?* That's a fair question, but it has some holes. The things we're proud of can vary greatly depending on our maturity. There was a time when I would've been proud to be a starving musician following my dreams—hopping from job to job—unwilling to sacrifice my passion for the sake of my family.

No doubt you've done some stupid things in your life of which you were pretty proud at the time. If nothing else, you were just proud to have had the balls to do it or proud to have been lucky enough to live through it.

Or maybe you've been proud of being the wrong kind of man: the strung-out rocker, the guy that has a different girl every few weeks, or the freeloader.

Most men have an inflated sense of self. We think more highly of ourselves than we ought. We think we look better than we do, that we're healthier and more fit than we actually are, that we're more important to our employer than reality would suggest, and that we're good enough to go to "the good place" when we die. So, asking ourselves whether or not we're a man we can be proud of may get a positive response whether it's befitting or not.

However, asking whether we're a man of merit is altogether different. To have merit means to be *deserving* of respect—other people's respect, not just our own. We can ask, *In what ways am I valuable to others?* or *In what ways can I say I truly do good towards others?* This question should be asked in every area of your life: work, home, family, marriage, and friendships.

The answer should be something like, *I see where I am doing well, and where I need to grow.* Before we can answer this question, however, we have to know what we're being judged against. What are the qualities that add merit to a man? What causes a man's fire to burn brightest? As we move farther into that dark cave in search of the truest tinder, how will we know when we find it?

In short, it is manly character that we're after, and character is derived either from our virtues or vices.

MANLINESS IS VIRTUE

Because power corrupts, society's demands for moral authority and character increase as the importance of the position increases.

JOHN ADAMS, FOUNDING FATHER, 2ND U.S. PRESIDENT, AND REBEL

Little time is spent on the topic of virtues in our present day and age. If you asked most men to name ten virtues, I'm inclined to believe they could not. I believe that's why a good man is hard to find. We don't think about or recognize goodness the same way we used to.

Yet, we long for it. We long to be that good man to which our wives and friends can turn when they need advice. We long to raise our sons and daughters to be good and to live rightly. We want to be proud of them, and we want them to be proud of themselves because they know they're making a worthwhile contribution to this world.

Living virtuously is a noble calling. To achieve it, we must begin to think virtuously and live by a set of principles that are timeless.

Virtue (Latin virtus)

- Manliness, manhood, virility
- Courage, resoluteness
- Goodness
- Character
- Excellence

As men, we must pursue virtues that are honored by both natural and supernatural law.

Developing Virtues in a Society that Values Knowledge

Virtue cannot be gained in the same manner as knowledge. It can't be taught and understood in the same manner as, say, mathematics or biochemistry. And herein lies the problem with modern society.

In the last century we have excelled at collecting, storing, cataloging, and retrieving information. That's not to say that we, as individuals, have more knowledge. As individuals, we're losing the game of knowledge because we have such quick access to information on the internet. We rarely practice committing things to memory as our forefathers once did.

It would be easy to make a case that the chief goal of mankind over the last many decades has been to collect and disseminate information. And yet as individuals we've lost something: wisdom gained from experience and our personal collection of knowledge.

At the same time, our focus on manly character has been severely diminished, resulting in the loss of at least two admirable traits of humanity in the pursuit of easily accessible data: wisdom and character.

Virtue is the True Test of Humanity

What separates us from animals? According to commonly held beliefs, it would boil down to our greater capacity to reason. Our minds are simply superior to those of any other living creature we have yet to encounter.

But is that what makes us truly separate from animals? If we accept this answer, we really wouldn't be separate, only smarter—essentially a smarter animal. I don't believe that to be true, and I don't believe you do either. In fact, I'll prove it's not simply our capacity for knowledge and ability to reason that separates us from the animals, and I'll do it using a most manly movie: *Terminator*.

In 1984, when I was seven years old and barely had a beard, a nude and perfectly sculpted Arnold Schwarzenegger exploded onto the screen like a Greek god robed in lightning, who, moments later, punched a hole through some punk with a nice jacket. *Terminator* was, and is, awesome!

More importantly, *Terminator* introduced me and millions of others to the concept of computers becoming so intelligent that they would become a threat to mankind. The idea that an advanced, artificial intelligence could unravel the secrets of time travel was simply a bonus that made for a cool storyline (and sequels...gotta have those).

Now, here is how I tie this in with virtues and humanity, though I really just want to write more about *Terminator*. Remember how the T-800 came out of the burning eighteen-wheeler? So awesome! Anyhow, if we truly believed that intelligence was what separated us from the animals, we would have rooted for the machines. Or at least we would have understood that they had a proper right to be on top of the food chain—if they needed food.

In fact, you probably never thought much about their superior intelligence and how it justified their actions. What upset us was the indiscriminate killing of innocent people—the thought of all that humanity had worked for being crushed under the titanium feet of soulless machines.

As viewers, we think about the children being raised underground. Children who were oppressed, the childhood they would never have, the peace they would never know, and a sun they would never see. The story is a nightmare that strikes directly at our hearts. It speaks to the fear that what makes us great—our virtues—is no match for intelligence.

It's a clever lie, but one we continue to believe. I know this because we seek to master intelligence before it masters us. In doing so, we leave what makes us human buried in the ashes of our ancestors.

All animals think, though humans do it far greater than any other. Machines can possess intelligence, and their ability to do so will increase on a scale that would make Skynet envious. As humans, however, we're the only ones who have a moral code—ethics—that goes beyond mere instinct or complex sets of data. Our moral code is affirmed by our ability to reason, but it springs from a source that isn't knowledge.

In other words, the acknowledgment of a moral rightness comes first, before knowledge of why a thing is right and why a thing is wrong. Therefore, to live a life primarily driven by knowledge—without the serious valuing of living virtuously—is to rob ourselves of our humanity. Or at the very least, it's to live as less of a human than we ought.

If we're neglecting our very humanity, how then can we expect to grow as men?

WHAT MAKES A VIRTUE A VIRTUE?

A man's character always takes its hue, more or less, from the form and color of things about him.

FREDERICK DOUGLASS, SOCIAL REFORMER, WRITER, AND STATESMAN

The question of what defines a virtue is a question as old as philosophy itself. When Socrates, Plato, and Aristotle began pondering the way we live, they wrestled with this very question.

They, like you and I, agreed that certain things appeared to be right and wrong from birth. But perhaps this was simply a result of where they had been raised and what they had been taught. They recognized a need to objectively look at their own manner of thinking—subjecting every "natural value" to suspicion—and to scrutinize the very meaning of what it means to be human.

The result? Socrates never reached a full definition of a virtue to which he could not pose a counterargument. At the same time, he held the simple belief that a man was to live virtuously because to be virtuous was to be good, and to do good was a supreme natural law to which man should adhere. Upon being accused of impiety—an unwillingness to be reverent or pious towards a deity—Socrates allowed himself to be executed because he believed it was good to accept the judgment of his community.

Aristotle, however, made more progress in defining a virtue. He considered it a "golden mean" between two extremes. Whereas Socrates viewed virtues as part of a universal law of good that would provide man with peace and alignment with nature itself, Aristotle's virtues were seen as a more individualistic duty and ultimately led to the chief pursuit of man: happiness. When Aristotle was accused of the same crime as Socrates, he fled. I consider this a smart move on his part as it's easier to find happiness when you're not six feet under!

Since the Enlightenment period of the eighteenth century, the question of whether or not a man can actually know good and evil has become one of broad speculation. Rather than attempt to tackle centuries of philosophical skepticism in this space, I'll briefly address an idea that has infected modern thought on virtues and morals and often leads people to think that there is no objective morality.

The Witch Burning Argument

The argument goes something like this: There are no moral absolutes because what is right for some is not right for others.

There was a time when people believed in witches. The belief was that by being in league with the devil, witches had the power to bring about terrible plagues, famine, and various diseases. While science has done a service to witches by absolving them of such malevolence, if science would have shown that witches were in league with the devil, then early witch burners would have been hailed as heroes.

In other words, no one believes that those who burned witches at the stake thought murder was morally acceptable. After all, in some instances the witches were accused of murder through the affliction of terrible and supernatural disease. They did, however, believe that killing a witch—being an earthly servant of the dark prince—was necessary to protect the larger community.

In this example we see several virtues clearly present: justice, love, consideration, responsibility, unity, piety, and righteousness. What we also see present in this example is something called *sociological behavior*, which is different from the moral principles themselves. This shows up in major atrocities wherever they occur.

Before Germany executed Jews in the Holocaust, they first dehumanized them. The same thing is happening in many Islamic societies today towards Jews as well as Americans and other citizens of Westernized nations. In fact, a quick search of U.S. World War I and World War II posters shows that we played that game as well when we dehumanized the people of Germany and Japan.

Because humans instinctively recognize murder as wrong, we must outweigh it with a greater moral reasoning: witches as being from the devil, Jews as pigs cursed by God, and America as the Great Satan. Society, then, buys into one moral principle as being more significant than another. In this way, immoral action is justified. In fact, throughout history we see the same moral principles represented in various societies. It takes the clever manipulation of a common moral code to achieve a collective goal through immoral means. Often, however, once the need for a particular cause—the taking of land, money, etc.—has passed, society will recognize and repent of its moral transgressions.

There's another way to look at the argument that there are no moral absolutes: from the perspective of the victim. If we think that Islamic terrorists believe it's acceptable to murder innocent people—and that it's evidence of relative morality—do you think the terrorist would welcome the thought of their children being murdered? Of course not! When we take the focus off the aggressor and instead look at the victim, we see moral truths very clearly. The excuses that justify the actions by a transgressor fall flat when they become the transgressed. In any case of persecution, we also see the great need for virtuous men to come to the aid of those who are not capable of standing their ground and defending their own.

Though I've used the terms moral and virtue interchangeably in the preceding section, there are slight differences between the two. Morals constitute a broader concept than a virtue. For example, the idea that "murder is wrong" is a moral. That moral may be made up of several virtues: respect for others, compassion, reverence, idealism, and wisdom. We might say, "There goes a man of good morals," or "There goes a man of good character," alluding to the same notion. When we talk about morals we are speaking of something good in a broad sense. Morals, however, can be vague and intermingled with tradition and sociological behavior, so it is best to consider virtues as the foundational building blocks of character.

THE GOLDEN MEAN

We are not studying in order to know what virtue is, but to become good, for otherwise there would be no profit in it.

ARISTOTLE, GREEK PHILOSOPHER

Aristotle held to the notion that a virtue was a golden mean between two extremes. For example, too much idealism can make a man high-minded and out-of-touch. But if idealism is balanced with simplicity, a harmony is achieved which results in a virtue: humility. Humility is the golden mean—or middle position—between the extremes of idealism and simplicity.

The complexity of the golden mean is why we're always growing and being refined as individuals. In fact, for millennia, Socratic philosophers have wrestled with how to go about practically defining character. That's why—and I can't believe I am about to write this—math may be able to help us out. Let me see if I can get the point across before we all fall into the nerd pit and this chapter is totally ruined.

The golden mean is another term for what mathematicians call the golden ratio. The golden ratio is a mysterious special number that appears in art, math, and architecture. What makes the golden ratio so interesting is that it's not simply a mathematical phenomenon. It's a geometric pattern evidenced in nature to such a significant degree that it's been called the *divine proportion*.

The architects of the Parthenon, sculptors of ancient Greek statues, and artists from the time of Leonardo da Vinci to Salvador Dalí have all utilized the golden ratio to accomplish one timeless objective: beauty. From the golden ratio we have derived the golden rectangle, the golden triangle, and the golden spiral. They each have an undeniable appeal of proportionality and symmetry.

And it's here that we find the brilliance in Aristotle's definition of a virtue as being the golden mean between traits of character. A virtuous man, a man of integrity, honor, patience, wisdom, temperance, and compassion—in other words, a man of good character—is, quite simply, a beautiful thing.

PRINCIPLES: THE WELL-SPRING OF VIRTUE OR VICE

A people that values its privileges above its principles soon loses both.

DWIGHT D. EISENHOWER,
34TH U.S. PRESIDENT AND FIVE-STAR GENERAL

When I was 10 years old I often rode shotgun in my granddaddy's truck because he took me to school in the mornings. We lived out in the country and so a ride to just about anywhere took a while. Looking back, I can see the blessing in those long drives.

My granddaddy would point out different types of trees. I was enamored by anything my hero was enamored with, so I learned to discern one type of tree from another and to eventually point them out myself. This fascination with different timbers has been with me most of my life and began on those early morning drives.

On one of those morning rides with my granddaddy, a police officer pulled him over for speeding. The officer was a young man in his twenties. My granddaddy, the consummate gardener, was wearing overalls, or at least, in my memory he is wearing overalls. The young officer issued a piece of paper to my grandad, and as the officer walked away, my hero invited the young man to look in the back of his truck. As so happened, we had a number of watermelons from our garden in the bed of the truck. Grandaddy gifted the young officer a watermelon, which he gladly accepted with a smile of true appreciation.

Knowing my grandaddy as I do, this was completely in character for him. He didn't give the young officer the gift to get out of a ticket or for any reason other than to share something good with a young man who might appreciate it. But it struck me then as it does now, just how rare a quality that is in a person. Guiding principles are one thing, but to have them at the ready—in a moment of inconvenience and possibly embarrassment—shows strength of an imitable character that few possess.

Principles are the values we hold as truth, upon which we make judgements as to whether something is good or bad. They're composed of our beliefs and are shaped by, and in turn, shape our worldview, our reasoning, and our means of rationalization. And, while we generally talk about principles in a positive light, it's possible to hold principles that lead not to virtue but to vice.

Let's use the virtue of frugality as an example—the virtue of being responsible and wise with money. A man who holds the principle, even unknowingly, that money means security—that having funds in the bank is associated with success and a man's worth—will tend towards the vices of being greedy, tightwadish, stingy, and miserly. Essentially, he will live life as a Scrooge because he fears losing money.

In contrast, a man who holds that money is important and that he should be responsible and accountable for its usage—a man who believes in compassion towards others and temperance in his own spending—will develop the virtue of frugality. While it may be hard to find a man who would say, *"I fear losing money because it affects how I feel about myself as a man,"* the way we live points to the principles we hold far more than the ideals we espouse.

I used the example of frugality because it is an area I have struggled with personally. I grew up two types of poor: country poor and city poor. Growing up in the country, we were poor, but we didn't feel poor. We grew our own food and we hunted. We had a well for water and plenty of space between us and our neighbors. I felt simple, but I rarely felt poor.

Being poor in a city, however, was a different experience. The trailer park was not as conducive to self-reliance, being so near the city where cash rules all. Those who are in poverty near a city, as I was, will feel it.

As I became an adult with a family of my own, I had a strong tendency to worry about finances and I longed for the ability to be more self-reliant. Those fears, ironically, led to poor financial decisions. It took a long time for me to recognize the difference between the principles I wanted to believe in—the principles that were in alignment with a fiscally wise man—and the principles by which I actually lived.

THE VIRTUES OF A MAN

As we consider the virtues a man ought to aspire to, we may wonder if there are virtues that apply more to men than they do to women. Are there values that apply particularly to manhood but not to womanhood? In short, no, but the way in which they are enacted is different, and there are certain virtues to which a man is drawn.

Integrity

Integrity is the first among manly virtues. Integrity is strengthened by the courage to stay true. Integrity ought to be a prized virtue among men. It takes great courage to be true, to be the man you claim to be, to keep your word, and to be known for not only your honesty, but for your love of truth. If a man cannot be trusted, he is less a man in every other respect.

Provider

The primary driving value of a man is to be a provider. We long to provide value, to provide protection, and to provide financially. For many of us, the instinct to provide really kicks in once kids enter the picture. An instinctive awareness comes over most men informing us that the world does not revolve around us, and that we're needed to raise a family. In order to be the provider that a growing family needs, a man must put on the virtues of discipline, industry, reliability, and excellence.

While women can also provide, their primary driver is to nurture. Note, I'm not saying men can't nurture or that women can't provide. Once again, virtues are for all. However, our biology will move us in the direction of coloring those virtues with different shades. When we recognize this and begin appreciating these differences, men will feel more like men and women will feel more like women.

Self-Reliance

A chief goal of a man is to be capable and self-reliant. This doesn't mean we never ask for help. On the contrary, we relish support from our brothers and long to support them, too, because this builds unity. However, we want to lessen our need and dependence upon others. We want to live in a society of capable men who choose to work alongside each other and add value to one another. The irony of self-reliance is that it begins with the virtue of humility. For each of us, our story begins on a blank page, and we fill it in as we go. As we journey, we take on the virtues of discernment, knowledge, and trustworthiness, among others.

Strength

It's no wonder that our heroes are shown to be strong, capable men. Though society has downplayed the importance of strength in the last few generations, men are designed to be strong. We're made to be the ones to which our wives turn to change a tire, split wood, load heavy stuff for the trip, carry in the bags, haul in the kill, and protect our families from danger. Strength ought to be prized among men and healthy competition and respect for strength should be the norm. In order to become strong, a man must develop the virtues of toughness, focused discipline, persistence, and ambition.

Building a Library of Call to Mind Examples

Most of our principles are defined during childhood, during a time when we're actively seeking meaning from the world and are trying to find our place in it. Once those tracks are laid down, however, we continue to follow them as adults, often unaware of where they're leading until it's too late.

In the small town of Mercer, Tennessee, where I grew up, our house sat on the banks of the Hatchie River and alongside an old railroad track. Though the tracks had been pulled up long before my time, the remnants of the railroad tracks still remained. As an adult, I've been out there with my boys and we still find railroad spikes and bolts with ease. Like the remains of that old railroad track, we may never be able to completely tear up the principles we picked up at an early age, but we can lay down some new principles—some new tracks—that will take us in a different, manlier direction in life. To do this we must first recognize what those old principles are. That will require some introspection and likely some input from others, as well.

As a boy, I found railroad spikes for some time before I knew what they were. After my granddaddy told me they were for a railroad, the whole history of that old area began to come alive in my imagination. Eventually, I would have figured it out on my own, but how nice and how rare to have someone in our lives who is willing to share with us a bit of wisdom at a time when we are willing to accept it.

For new principles to be laid down, we need examples of those principles being lived out which are greater than the examples we lived in. It's most effective if those examples come from other men whom we respect and regularly meet and work with, but helpful examples can come from men of history as well.

When I was growing up, time management was never a focus on either side of my family. This allowed for a good deal of spontaneity, which was a plus, but it also allowed for a good bit of wasted time and boredom. Years ago, if you had asked me if I believed time management was important, I would have said yes. But if you looked at my life you would've seen a young man who had neither the skills nor the beliefs to match. I lived as though life would wait for me—that goals would be accomplished while I enjoyed an impulsive and unencumbered life.

To correct my view of time management, I needed to see the principles lived out as well as the fruits of those principles. I observed this first in my wife who takes to scheduling like a fish to water. But that did not cause me to change. Instead, I developed something of a frustrated reliance on her as the manager of my time. As the years went by and I grew as a man, I read about Benjamin Franklin's scheduling practices and then the excellent time management of so many men I admired—some I knew personally and some I only knew through stories. The principle of time management began to align with the rightness and the practice of it and I began to live out that principle in my life. Iron sharpens iron.

A lot of men feel like they're betraying their family or their heritage when they begin to head down a road that looks different from the one they've traveled for so long. When we look for better ways of doing things and living our lives, it can feel like we're turning our backs on those who cared for us for so long.

Yet, in order to grow, we must head further into that dark cave where the truest timber lies. We must leave those old tracks and find our new heading. We must blaze a few new trails and feel our way around in the dim. One day when we're feeling rather worn out from the journey, we might come back to those old tracks only to find them rusty and narrow. Then we'll realize they're from our old life, and that we've outgrown them.

6

LIVING TRUTHFULLY

All truths are easy to understand once they are discovered; the point is to discover them.

GALILEO GALILEI, ITALIAN ASTRONOMER, PHILOSOPHER, AND MATHEMATICIAN

All men are explorers, and some, discoverers. During the age of the Great Arctic Explorers, men of renown such as Robert Falcon Scott, Earnest Shackleton, and Roald Amundsen—along with their teams of hardy and often hairy men—braved the most inhospitable and remote points on earth for the sake of discovery and the honor which is bestowed upon those who have witnessed firsthand some undeniable truth about their world.

Before setting off, the men would consult with other explorers who had made previous attempts, often spending years planning their expedition. They put their trust in the character of their colleagues, the accuracy of their estimations, the dependability of their equipment, and the trueness of their course, for they knew that no manner of daring, courage, or hardihood could sway the bitter cold reality into which they were going to embark.

Exploration and discovery are still taking place today, and I'm often fascinated by the reports of some new shipwreck or treasure found. In

2013 the journal of George Murray Levick—a member of Robert F. Scott's fatal Terra Nova Expedition—was found only yards from one of the team's campsites at the South Pole, preserved under the ice until a recent warming brought it to the surface. Levick and the other survivors of the expedition team left for home in 1913, making the discovery a timely 100 years after that heroic and tragic march to the South Pole. Though most men will never hunt for sunken pirate treasure or set off to the ends of the globe, every man is an explorer, and all that we discover, we become.

Our convictions stem from our principles, but our principles are only as good as they are true. In life, we are tested, and thus our principles either line up to the reality of the world in which we live and are hardened—becoming a sure foundation—or else they are exposed as being false. Though false principles may be well-intentioned, they cannot support the hard work of a man which life demands.

Unfortunately, we're stubborn and often want to hold on to our beliefs even when they've been shown as untrue or naïve. We tend to surround ourselves with like-minded individuals who parade along with us in our ignorance and guileless bliss. Unchallenged and attending to core beliefs without merit, we can't move forward in life. The foundation for growth as a man—as a husband, as a father, as a leader—must be strong enough to bear the weight of marriage, children, communities, and friendships, all with love and patience and wisdom, and far too often, when we stand alone in our convictions.

BECOMING A MAN OF CONVICTION

The end goal of living truthfully is to become a man of deep conviction. Men of the sort of conviction that has been tested and honed, are stable forces for positive change in their homes and friendships. They are sought after as mentors and leaders to give trustworthy advice, represent a cause, and take the right course of action even when that action may be unpopular. Unlike most of the politicians we witness, they do not check the direction of the wind before sharing their thoughts. Rather, they rely on the principle of honesty, believing that an honest man who may end up being wrong is more likely to be forgiven than a liar caught in his deceptions.

While we frequently witness a number of impassioned people responding to an incident or cause, we don't often witness men of conviction as we once did. Though a sincere opinion may be extolled with great fervor, a man of conviction has a rationale to his beliefs that goes beyond the emotional. He grounds his credence in reality. A man who speaks and acts from emotion alone is likely to be easily shaken. His convictions will come across as harsh, and he'll be easily offended.

There is something else to be said about the man of iron conviction: he has a peace about him. No doubt this is one of the qualities that draw people to him and, almost instinctively, people put their trust in him. For the man who has sought after truth and then tested his findings, there is a sense of calm that covers others like a blanket and shield. He, himself, is guarded against the distracting barbs of the world and he tends only to the problems which he has deemed important.

He lives his life as a skilled craftsman, putting his hand to the plane and working an issue until it's leveled and may be put to good use. He knows that the end result of his work will be judged by a keener eye—the Master Craftsman—and all measurements, cuts, joints, and fit will either reflect the work of a man growing in his own mastery—however novice he may be when his end comes—or that of a man who never cared for the trueness of his cuts or the precision of his measurements.

The man of conviction became such a man because he first believed—in some great or small way—in doing work and doing it well. I've found that becoming such a man often requires an initial posturing of oneself in ways that are contrary to the nature of most men. Humility and openness being the important qualities of a man wishing to become something more than he currently finds himself.

Reason: The Road to Manly Conviction

In order to become a man of conviction, we need to not only increase our knowledge of the things we believe are right, but we must also know what right is. In other words, how do we know *truth* when we find it? And how can we know there is such a thing as truth to begin with?

Truth is simply defined as a proposition which corresponds to the way the world is. A common example would be the proposition "All men are mortal." Though we have not seen all men and can't know this to be one hundred percent true, we have enough experiential knowledge—also called inductive reasoning—to come to a reasonable conclusion. The test to determine whether this proposition is true is the common observation of the death of every man. Aside from Christ—who was not simply a mortal and does not fit the premise—we have no recorded evidence of a human who lives forever.

There is another form of reasoning called deductive reasoning which starts the whole process in the reverse order than inductive reasoning. Deductive reasoning must still correspond to reality to be considered truth. Let's use Sherlock Holmes as an example here, notably most famous for his use of deductive reasoning. Suppose Sherlock steps into a crime scene which has Scotland Yard baffled. He notices a shoeprint from which he gauges the suspect was male, 180 pounds—oh excuse me, twelve stone and twelve—and six feet tall with a slight limp. Thus, he concludes the suspect is a veteran with a war injury.

Sherlock began with the evidence and formed a proposition about the suspect. When he catches the suspect—and he will because he is

Sherlock Holmes—he will see that his proposition corresponds with reality. He will then scold the imbeciles at Scotland Yard, and another case will be solved. To be fair, Sherlock is actually using both inductive and deductive reasoning. We cannot deduce things without some prior understanding of how the world actually works. Sherlock has to assume that a shoe size corresponds to the size of a foot, that foot size often corresponds to height, and that the impression depth of the shoe print corresponds to weight and so forth.

The point here is that anything we identify as truth must relate back to the world as it actually is, not merely as we want it to be. And while we cannot solely rely on our personal experience to make such a determination, we also cannot discount our own observances of natural law as to how the world operates.

Reasoning in the Absence of Natural Law

Since the industrial age of the 1800s, men have undergone a massive shift in our relationship to natural law. Prior to the assembly line and mechanized manufacturing, men were apprenticed artisans. A cobbler, for example, made the entire shoe. He procured the leather and stitching, the polish, the tacks, the tools for cutting, and all the instruments of his trade. He took the order and crafted a shoe to the specifications of his customer. He was wholly skilled in the process, and the product you received was crafted by an artisan with all of the detail and attention a man gives to a shoe that would bear his name and his handiwork.

Enter the assembly line of the industrial age. In an assembly line, a man, woman, or child cuts or stitches part of a shoe. In many cases they are simply lining up some raw material, pulling a lever, and letting a machine do the work. They do this hundreds of times a day for customers they will never meet. Don't get me wrong, I am not saying industrialization is altogether bad, but we have lost something in our progress. We have lost a connection with natural law. Let me explain.

Natural law is the belief that there are common truths inherent in nature and the life we all live that can be discovered through common reason and by observing the way the world works. Natural law doesn't simply deal with nature in the way we think of nature today. While natural law tells us that bees like flowers and fish like worms—truths we can discern through observation (inductive reasoning)—natural law also deals with larger principles that form the foundation of human rationale. Take the U.S. Declaration of Independence for instance:

> *"We hold these truths to be* ***self-evident****, that all men are created equal, that they are endowed by their Creator with certain unalienable Rights, that among these are Life, Liberty and the pursuit of Happiness."*

The founders of this new America staked their lives, fortunes, and sacred honor on a belief in a self-evident truth. They believed it was true not only for Englishmen of the age but also for men of any age or nation.

So, what does this have to do with the cobbler and the industrial age? When men are closer to nature, when we have our hands and lives bound to it, we are steeped in natural law. The cobbler knows that his success depends upon the quality of his product, the care for his customers, and even the cows from which his leather comes. In his work, he learns the rewards of patience. In the managing of his business, he learns the value of a dollar. In the repairing of soles, he knows the strain of each of his customer's work. He knows that boys will wear out a pair of shoes much faster than girls. He knows that hard work pays, but that smart work often pays better. He is intimately familiar with certain truths upon which other truths may be built, and thus his ability to reason is built up as well. Whether or not he takes up the opportunity to build his reasoning skills is up to him, but it's important that he has some foundation.

For many in modern society, the experience of natural law is severely lacking. Not only do we not work the land or hunt in the ways we used to, but even the most mundane of tasks have been outsourced to others: mowing our lawns, growing and processing our food, building and maintaining our homes, the educating of our children, our personal safety, our careers, and so on. In each area that we have outsourced to someone else, we have lost something in the trade-off.

In most cases, we have lost the natural truths which are taught in the process of work. This leaves many men with a narrow foundation on which to build their reasoning capabilities. Thus, when a smooth-talking politician, evangelist, or salesman comes to town and starts making promises in exchange for votes and dollars, we are too easily taken in. When social issues of the day come about, we are more fragmented in our response because our society does not have the root principles of rusticity and work on which we have been built. Thus, we have varying extremes on views for issues that were not an issue at all fifty years ago. And we have no clear path to a resolution because of the breakdown of common reason.

How Do We Recover Natural Reasoning and Common Sense?

There's little chance that, as time progresses, we are going to revert to more of an agrarian culture or have less automation in our lives. There may be periods (*Come on apocalypse! I'm not hoarding for nothin!*) but there will likely be more automation in the future and less hands-on work.

I liken the current situation to that of the Physical Culture which began to take root in the late 1800s. As people made the move from rural to urban areas, they spent more time sitting at a desk than working on their feet. The notion of exercise for health began to take hold. Men took to gyms to learn how to care for their bodies. When culture moved swiftly towards machination and ease, it became necessary to exercise for the sake of health because they lacked the natural benefits of hard work.

In much the same way, it is necessary to do some things by hand, which could be automated, for the sake of our humanity. It is necessary to have our boots (or toes) in the mud on occasion, and to shake a few carrots loose from the soil. It is good for a man to behold grander views than that of his neighborhood or cityscape. It is good for a man to ponder his smallness—and yet his uniqueness—in the world. It is good to marvel at the grand design and give credit to the Designer.

This notion resonates with those of my generation and possibly a few more afterwards, but it may be lost on those who are too far separated from the enigmatic satisfaction of soil and sweat. This is where you and I come in. Our job, as men, is to carry forward the torch and to be that light in the woods that other men see and wonder, *What is he doing that I am not?*

I can't help but think back to the many stories I have heard from other men about their grandfathers—most notably men from the Greatest Generation. As boys they were often indifferent to the lessons grandpa taught—he was just being grandpa. But as men, they look around and see fewer men of grandpa's caliber and consider how the world is the worse for it. To them, grandpa is the light in the distance. Though he may be gone, his embers remain in the hearts and minds of his children and grandchildren.

Allow me to tie this illustration in with that of nature, for I feel I have not done a good job in that regard. Industriousness is a virtue, yet for many it's an abstract notion of diligent and intelligent work. But, for those who knew grandpa, *he* was industry. He was boldness, he was willpower, he was selflessness, he was honesty, he was strength, and so on. The concept of a virtue became embodied in a person: grandpa.

Similarly, nature is becoming an abstraction. Nature is ecology, is biodiversity, is organic, and is a tamed force to which man has no lasting connection. Yet for a man who has experienced nature, it is life, it is the smell of dirt, it is the grand old tree you talked to when you were a boy, and its sounds are the whispers of a friend. It is not tame, and it is always instructing. It's the difference between knowledge of a thing and truly knowing a thing. The difference between an acquaintance and a friend.

Let us have one hand in the soil and another on the console if we must, but let us not remove ourselves so far from nature that the very basis of truth is foreign to us.

The Role of Religion in Rational Thought

While society continues to increase the divide between reason and religion, philosophers bridge the two, knowing that it is from the very questions which religions attempt to answer that we have a number of quandaries to which we make every effort to solve with a logical explanation. Why is there something rather than nothing? What constitutes morality? Is there purpose to life? Do humans have a soul? How can we identify the start of life? What defines personhood? Are God-given rights a real thing?

Though the religions of the world differ on the answers to these questions, that doesn't mean religion should be discounted. Rather, religion ought to be subjected to reason. After all, faith is a wonderful virtue to possess, but how much better is it when that faith is also found to be a reasonable belief? The challenge is that not all religions stand the test of reason even if they have tenets which are valuable and should not be discarded. For example, many religions hold the belief that children should respect their parents. Though they may arrive at this station by different roads, many of which would put a thinking man in the ditch, the conclusion is sound. Therefore, we must test both the soundness of the religion itself and its teachings as separate things.

In Search of the Known-Unknown

You know a movie from your boyhood was amazing when you remember scenes as an adult. Often, a new meaning emerges from what you assumed was past and settled. I've noticed this when watching a movie from my childhood with my teenage sons. There is so much more happening than I was able to realize when I first saw it, and so much more meaning packed into two hours of boyhood bliss than my naïve self could have comprehended.

I think, as men, we learn to hold onto moments and scenes and, because we are older and have a history of our own, stories touch on our hearts much more deeply than is possible in our youth. As I was putting this chapter together, my mind kept pulling up images of *Indiana Jones*. I've done enough writing to recognize when there is something hidden in my subconscious that's trying to bubble up to the surface, and to neither press for it—which our shy hidden-self views as a violation of sorts—nor to go chasing after it. If I allow the thought to come in time through a sort of mental and emotional dance—a tease here, a wondering there—eventually it will come out of the shadows and make itself known.

I was led to one of the final scenes in *The Last Crusade*. On a quest which his father began, Indy is forced by Nazis and a betraying friend, Walter

Donovan, into an ancient and hidden canyon-side cavern known as the Temple of the Sun. Indy must pass a series of deadly trials to reach the Holy Grail—the legendary cup of Christ. It was believed that anyone who drinks from the Holy Grail will be granted immortal life. For Donovan, this is a chance for immortality. For Indy, however, it's the only chance to save the life of his father who has been fatally shot. If you've seen the film, you know that what comes next is pure movie gold. Indy passes the trials, and Donovan, along with his lovely comrade Dr. Elsa Schneider, follows him into a chamber where they expect to find the Grail. Instead, they're greeted by an ancient Templar knight—a guardian of the Grail. It appears there will be one more trial. Rather than the one Holy Grail, they find a myriad of false chalices spread before them. They must choose a cup and drink from it. If they choose wisely, they may leave. If they choose poorly, well, it doesn't turn out so good.

Both men—Indiana Jones and Walter Donovan—have been in search of something they believe to exist, yet they find themselves faced with the reality that they don't really know the thing for which they have sought. They have searched for the known-unknown. They would have only been able to come this far had they some knowledge to lead them there. Both men are right in their understanding up to a point. It is at this junction, however, that they part ways and their decisions make all the difference.

Lusting for power, Donovan is determined to go first, but he cannot bring himself to make a selection. Dr. Schneider offers to choose a cup for him, and he agrees. Dr. Schneider, who really has the hots for Indiana—I mean come on, Indy has a tan, a fedora, a perpetual five-o-clock shadow, defies death on a daily basis, plus he's American—selects a golden goblet encrusted with jewels and hands it to Donovan.

"*This certainly is the cup of the King of Kings,*" Donovan says, dipping the goblet in water. He drinks, feels a tingling sensation, and then ages to death right before our eyes.

"*He chose—poorly*," the knight—whom I like to call Sir Fredrick the Obvious—calmly pronounces.

Now it's Indy's turn. His selection is the exact opposite of Donovan's. He chooses a worn and battered clay cup, exclaiming, "*That's the cup of a carpenter*." A few seconds after he drinks from the cup, the knight says, "*You have chosen—wisely*."

That these men had made different decisions with different consequences I understood as a child. When you're eleven years old, it's a memorable event to see a man rot away and be eaten by worms on the big screen. What had eluded me was the *why* behind the different choices. I believe it was this: Walter Donovan knew only of the *glory* of Christ, whereas Indiana knew something of the *man* of Christ. The glory to which Donovan no doubt was drawn could have belonged to any number of heralded figures, but the glory which belonged to Christ came through the life and sacrifice of a layman. In the end, the truth freed one man while an incomplete or false belief destroyed the other.

As we peer through the window of this illusory tale, I believe we can observe a few very real truths.

First, men can seemingly aspire towards the same goal, though with very different purposes. Often the true intent of their aspirations is hidden even from themselves. A science-minded man may desire to know the world through a greater understanding of how the world works. He believes, quite rightly, that a great deal of good can be achieved in solving the riddles of the natural world. He desires to answer the questions that he does not yet know to ask, and he is aware of this grand undertaking.

The man of religion and philosophy is appreciative of the *how* but desires to know the essence or form of things beyond the material. He wants to grasp the immaterial nature of things—to know the value of things beyond their substantive worth. He takes the *how* and uses rationale to derive the *why* only to discover that there is also a *who.*

Second, both men must be tested. More accurately, both approaches must be tested. The man who carries in his mind a love of wisdom—both scientific and philosophical—should challenge his beliefs regularly. The generation which misses the mark by a little, may find the next generation proudly donning swastikas.

GETTING YOUR BEARING

Set your course by the stars, not by the lights of every passing ship.

GENERAL OMAR N. BRADLEY, U.S. ARMY GENERAL

Most men are never taught to think critically, nor do they acquire the skills of rational thinking by which they might process an ever-broadening and connected world of ideas. To remain as such is to allow one's self to be pushed along, like an unguided ship at sea, by the winds and whims of society. You will go with the flow, but you may not reach your intended destination.

In order for us to direct our course, we must first get our bearings. As in the nautical realm, getting your bearings in life means determining your position based upon two or more known points. If you're lost in the woods with a map, you can determine your position by examining the nearby terrestrial features: a stream to your left or a large hill up ahead.

Applying this principle to life, however, is more difficult. Typically, a man has only one well-known point to which he can compare his current position, namely, how he grew up. Our tendency is to either break from the ways in which our family operated—believing it was false and not conducive to a good life—or to embrace it wholeheartedly—unwilling to question the ways in which our family taught us to think and approach life.

While it's good to know how our family dynamics shape us, it limits us to a singular point of reference from which we can only gauge how much we are—or are not—like our parents. To become a man of conviction, we need to know where we stand as an independent being, beholden to our own beliefs in a sea of ideas and pressures to conform. Our convictions are a guiding force for our lives and those whom we influence. As such, a proper understanding of where we are and where we are headed is critical for our success.

It stands to reason that the more points of reference we have the better we can assess our bearings. But how does a man go about getting more reference points? How does one discover the figurative hills and valleys and streams all about him?

The Learned Man

One of the interesting aspects of getting your bearings in life is that our current position is not defined only by our presence in a particular culture, but also our location in time, on the timeline of human history. As such, we can read about the lives of men and women who came before us to determine how we have arrived in our particular culture with all of its beliefs.

We can determine what has worked and what has not, in order that we might find our bearings and chart our course accordingly. In other words, our knowledge of past events, as well as current events, provide us points of reference. In order to grow in this area, a man needs to develop a love of learning and cultivate an appreciation for ideas that are foreign to him. A love of reading and learning on many different topics must be the tilth of a man's soul wherein new points of reference are planted, nurtured, and raised in the garden of the mind and spirit.

Elihu Burritt—The Learned Blacksmith

Born in Connecticut in the year 1810 as the youngest of a family of ten children, Elihu Burritt is a testament to a man whose mind and body were actively engaged in rewarding activity. At the age of sixteen, Elihu's father died, leaving him as the provider of his family. While he apprenticed his body to the art of metalsmithing, he apprenticed his mind by reading any book he could get his hands on.

Before his father died, a young Elihu tended the forge and chores on their small farm, and he readily took to the work. However, as was often the case in his day, school took a backseat to his duties at home. But Burritt would not allow the lack of classroom instruction to hinder his pursuits of knowledge. As he blew the bellows, he would work out complex arithmetic problems in his head—unable to take a free moment to write them down—then check his sums later that night. Similarly, he made use of his downtime endeavoring to learn various languages and information of any kind. I'll copy a few lines from his private diary here, which I have borrowed from James Parton's work *Captains of Industry*:

> *"Monday, June 18. Headache; 40 pages Cuvier's Theory of the Earth; 64 pages French; 11 hours forging."*

> *"Tuesday, June 19. 60 lines Hebrew; 30 pages French; 10 pages of Cuvier; 8 lines Syriac; 10 lines Danish; 10 lines Bohemian; 9 lines Polish; 15 names of stars; 10 hours forging."*

> *"Wednesday, June 20. 25 lines Hebrew; 8 lines Syriac; 11 hours forging."*

Elihu's love of learning never ceased with age, and his wisdom on a number of issues is one of marvel to this day. He wrote over thirty-five books in his lifetime. He was appointed Consul to Birmingham England by President Lincoln, and he was an inspirational figure to many—the epitome of the American self-made man.

We can see in the life of Elihu Burritt the power of a determined will and the wise usage of time and resources to accomplish a goal. It has been reported that he once walked one hundred miles from Connecticut to Boston in search of books to further his education. In any case, educating one's self was far more difficult for Elihu than it is for us. As one admirer of Mr. Burritt said after hearing of his account, *"It is enough to make one who has good opportunities for education hang his head in shame."*

If You Want to Grow, Read

The men of admirable character and conviction whom history is obliged to recount, have, by and large, had a voracious appetite for books. For some figures, such as Elihu Burritt and Theodore Roosevelt, an active mind is apparent in their earliest records. It may lead us to believe that we're either born with it or we're not.

But like any muscle, the mind can be strengthened. I have found in myself that a maturity of mind didn't come until I was in my late twenties, and I didn't have a serious desire for books until I was in my thirties. Though I have always loved stories, I would not have considered myself a reader for most of my life.

The histories of others, the impact of their legacies, the beliefs of ages past, and the consequences of those beliefs all provide insight as to how we came to be in the culture in which we find ourselves. As such, we use these points of history to determine our color on the spectrum of worldviews. Not only can we determine our stance in the arena of ideas by reading books, but we can adjust our position according to the dictates of our beliefs.

Living in Pursuit of Truth

Perhaps the greatest obstacle to a man living a life in pursuit of the noble moniker "an honest man" is the subtle and persuasive powers of a lie he tends to believe. The lie is simple in its arrangement as it has two primary components which make it alluring: it is self-serving and unbinding.

The lie serves the one who tells it or believes it, and it seemingly unfetters the man to the otherwise restraints of truth. He is now free to sleep with that other woman, play the corporate game to get ahead, or lash out in anger when his kids have it coming. Yet, for the man who desires to be governed by principles over passions and charts his course for Mansville, his guideposts are truth, and wisdom his reward. In the cave he finds his footing sure when truth is his foundation. In his fire burns the hardy pith of the ancient oaks, brought up in good soil and the light of the ages.

Conviction forms in a man when belief is tested, and, like the jack pines of the north, the harsh winter does not steal his green. The great winds may shake him, but his roots hold fast. Once he is well seasoned, he knows by instinct when the weather is shifting, and he bears gusts and gales alike, standing true and straight and confident in the passing of life's storms.

Men who live truthfully—men with the courage of conviction—are sorely needed in an age of image-bearers and salesmen of deceit. The quest for truth is a noble undertaking in which a man is honor-bound to acknowledge his false beliefs and admit his wrongs. Wisdom he discovers, and wise he will become.

7

LIVING SPIRITUALLY

There are no ordinary people. You have never talked to a mere mortal. Nations, cultures, arts, civilization—these are mortal, and their life is to ours as the life of a gnat. But it is immortals whom we joke with, work with, marry, snub, and exploit—immortal horrors or everlasting splendors.

C.S. LEWIS, CHRISTIAN AUTHOR AND APOLOGIST

When a man begins to live his life deliberately, to seek goodness and truth, and has within him the courage to accept what he finds, I believe he will find himself at the foot of the cross of Christ.

When he has carried the torch to light the dark, hidden recesses of his soul, knows the width and breadth of his cave, and has heaved the old timbers on the fire of his heart, he will ask himself, *Who has put these here? Who has stored them away within me? Who is it that struck the match and fanned the flames of my spirit?*

He will begin to see some forethought to it all—some planning and purpose. And when he begins to believe there's a great plan at work, the fire within him will burn all the more brightly.

In order for us to live spiritually, we must first see ourselves as spiritual beings. This will be harder for some men than for others due to upbringing, experience with religion, and the worldview they've formed up to this point in their lives. To recognize ourselves as a spirit means we must acknowledge there is an unseen world at play. A world that is just as real as the one we inhabit but possibly more permanent and more powerful. A world that is strange and yet familiar. A world to which more of our true self belongs.

AWARENESS OF THE ETERNAL

We are told in the biblical book of Ecclesiastes that God has "placed eternity in the hearts of men." Be still for a moment. Listen. Don't you feel this to be true? Our hearts testify to another realm—a reality glinted and then gone when the corporeal endeavors to resolve with the spiritual.

We see throughout history that humans have always—regardless of tribe or location—had an inkling of a world beyond this one. There's always been a notion of some distant place where our natures are ferried away while our bodies remain here. There is an inborn awareness of the eternal, not only as a concept, but as a reality—a reality that is particularly bound to ourselves and one another.

Some would say that this concept of an afterlife is just an attempt by our subconscious to resolve our fear of a final state of nonexistence. But wouldn't an easier resolution be that we are simply gone? To accept that we lived for a time and then were no more? It would be a type of torture for our minds to have crafted a fictional world where parents and friends and lovers go to wait until we're reunited. To think we would live all of our remaining years in hope for a hereafter of which we can never be fully convinced, yet build our worldview around, dictate our lives by, only for it to be a figment of the unconscious mind is a dreadful lunacy. That is, unless it's true.

The 19th-century minister, Alexander Maclaren, speaks to this:

> Transiency is stamped on all our possessions, occupations, and delights. We have the hunger for eternity in our souls, the thought of eternity in our hearts, the destination for eternity written on our inmost being, and the need to ally ourselves with eternity proclaimed by the most short-lived trifles of time. Either these things will be the blessing or the curse of our lives. Which do you mean that they shall be for you?

The practice of denying our inmost being is far too commonplace and easy these days. The mind which looks inward to the heart is the one which is not being distracted by the constant pull of the outside world. In this age, it can be uncomfortable to be alone and to be still enough to hear the ancient words written on your soul.

By being still enough I don't mean being motionless, sitting down in some meditative trance. I am talking about an emotional stillness—a quietness of the spirit. For most men, this stillness comes through rote work or exercise. When the body stays busy and the mind is free to contemplate, a man is able to explore the caverns of his spirit. There used to be ample time for this type of meditative work. Splitting and stacking firewood, hunting, gardening, tending to the fields and animals, and a walk or ride to town—they all provided the type of steady, dull work that allowed our minds to wander *and* to wonder.

In this type of setting a man could explore his inmost self, think thoughts about thoughts, and on occasion, usually without warning, have a momentary glimpse of his own spirit.

MEMENTO AETERNUM

In the circles of manhood and stoicism is often seen or heard the popular phrase, *Memento Mori*, which is Latin for "Remember Death" or "Remember Mortality." The goal is to bring awareness to our own mortality. It's a timely reminder for a culture that is not as familiar with the reality of death as past generations. In an age of emotional fragility and rational frailty, the pendulum of stoicism is working to swing us back to center. But, I believe there is a better way of seeing things and thinking about who we are and who we are becoming.

Memento Aeternum—Remember Eternity

In recent generations, I've noticed a disproportionate focus on perfecting the big decisions in life: Where should I go to college? What should I study? When should I get married? Should I get married? How do I know if I've found the right person?

In our grandparent's or great grandparent's day, a person's options for the big decisions in life were rather limited. Or at least we can say that the world seemed like a smaller place, and so the education, careers, and love life options also appear limited. Family was more important, travel was more difficult, and the types of careers were not as diverse as they are now. So, you remained loyal and close to your family. The result is that you were likely to marry a sweet girl in town, take up a local job, and head down a path which was not too different from others in your community. You would have done much of this because "it's just what you do." You got married in a church, settled down, worked hard to bring home the bacon, went to church on Sundays, raised a family, and looked forward to retirement.

This is no longer the case. Nearly any passion you have can be turned into a profitable career or business. This doesn't mean that the road to success is as clearly marked as you may like, but the fact that it is possible to make a living by following your passions causes many to question traditional career decisions. Who wants to be saddled up to a job for forty years when they could be doing something they truly love and are inspired by?

This raises a problem that most generations past have not had to address: We have so many options but very few choices. In other words, the potential for who we could be and what we could do are seemingly unlimited, but we can only test a few paths and ultimately settle on one. Due to the constraints of time, the rest of our career options will be left untried. There are dreams we'll never realize. Happiness that we'll never taste. For a generation that wants to drink life to the lees, it seems to be a terrible truth that we will all leave some grapes on the vine.

The same can be said for love. Sure, that girl you met is nice and all, but what if there is someone better? What if you say "*I do*" and the next week you meet your soulmate? What if you learn something about yourself ten years from now that changes who you want to be, what drives you, or what you find attractive in another person? What if you wake up one day and think, *I don't want this life?*

These are not irrational concerns. In fact, everything I've mentioned happens fairly regularly. However, at the heart of all of our decision avoidance is a prevailing fear: *"What if I miss my one opportunity in this life to do what I really ought to be doing?"* Which is another way of asking, *"What if I miss my one chance at happiness?"*

Along with the increasing number of paths for love and career, there is an additional pressure that we see in our time that has further complicated the decision-making process: social media. Granted, while people have always felt pressure to conform to societal norms, they typically did so within a smaller community sphere that generally shared the same values and opinions. Having two or three people who do not agree with who you married or how successful you are isn't the same as two to three hundred—or two to three thousand. While the freedom to be who you are is greater than ever before, there's also pressure to ensure who you are is shareable and likeable.

In one sense, the spiritually minded man has always had some view of this. The audience of souls with which we will be eternally in community with, dwarfs any count of fans and followers he may achieve here. The difference, however, is that a spiritual view puts things in the proper perspective and leads to a type of freedom with others rather than anxiety to align with the ever-shifting particularities of society. While we all long for a community in which to belong and a family in which we're known and loved, those who have their focus on the here and now find themselves struggling for connection and wholeness. For Christians, this sense of belonging has already been achieved. We only need to recognize it and accept it.

The perspective shift is profound. Yours is not an eighty-year life. Stop acting as if you have this short span in which to achieve something profound. Greater things await. There will come a day when your time here—the career, the marriage, and the success—will all be as a blink of an eye. Don't get me wrong, you should work hard and do good under the sun, but do so with a sense of freedom from time, not enslavement to it.

Memento Aeternum—remember that you are eternal.

A KINGDOM OF ENDS

Act in such a way that you treat humanity, whether in your own person or in the person of another, always at the same time as an end and never simply as a means.

IMMANUEL KANT, PRUSSIAN GERMAN PHILOSOPHER

We live in a kingdom of ends. Each person you meet has a home in the mind of the Creator. Too often we treat one another as merely a random acquaintance that can be used to accomplish some felt desire: sex, money, success, fame, ego, and so forth. A man who lives with an awareness of the spiritual, however, must recognize the bestowed and incalculable worth of everyone he meets.

The Creator of all has put his mark on you and me. Each of us is, as Kant says, an end in and of ourselves. People are never simply a means to achieving something else. God said that we are meant for a relationship with Him and one another in the everlasting courts of His home. This should not only move us towards the Golden Rule—treat others as you wish to be treated—it's a good and rational way of living. It creates a culture where respect for one another is the norm. I believe we can always use more of this.

In considering the spiritual and making a regular habit of thinking of others as fellow commuters with whom we will journey to an enduring station, we recognize that our legacy will not have a transient stop. The effect we have on others is not simply bound to the world in which we reside—not even to time. There is a Book in which good deeds are recorded and forever remembered, and there is a place where you will see the souls of your neighbors as they truly are. In light of this, how would a man live? How should a man consider his legacy or what legacy really is?

I believe that even if a man were to envision an empire and have the capability of creating it, he would be small-minded in this regard. A true legacy is not an empire in all its glory, for even empires fall. Rather, it is a tilling of the ground, a true word by the fire, an eye of reassurance, a tear for a tear, and standing shoulder to shoulder with those who might otherwise stand alone.

In our Kingdom of Ends, small moments endure.

MUST I BE A CHRISTIAN TO BE A GOOD MAN?

There is an assumption that most Christian men's ministries make which is rarely ever explained to a non-Christian: In order to be a good man you also need to be a follower of Christ. But is this true? Can you be a good man without being a Christian?

To answer this properly, we need to ensure we mean the same thing when we use the words Christian and good.

What Is a Christian?

In its simplest terms, a Christian is someone who believes in Jesus Christ as their Lord and Savior and who has committed their life to Him. Without context, however, that definition doesn't help us much. Lord and Savior of what exactly?

A Christian believes that God created mankind, but that we separated ourselves from God through sin. Sin simply means "missing the mark." What is the mark? According to God, it's perfection. Our failure to live a perfect life has put us at odds with the Creator of all things. The result is alienation from God.

If you're new to this notion, it can sound a bit harsh. After all, no one is perfect. It seems to be an impossible standard to begin with followed by an overly severe judgment by God. However, consider this for a moment. You and I have done things in our life that we regret. We've fallen short of the mandates of our own conscience and grieved our hearts over the thoughts and actions that do not live up to our own standards. And our standards are not that high. In truth, we have never known perfection. We merely have a concept of it, but we have never experienced it.

God, however, is perfect. He experiences perfection as a state of being. If we, who are fairly lenient on our own failings and have a low standard of expectations, still feel ashamed of ourselves from time to time, how much more does God experience this?

Thankfully, this is where Jesus comes in. He was the embodiment of God in human form. He lived a perfect life and sacrificed himself on our behalf. The punishment we deserve was attributed to His death, which He did not deserve. He paid a penalty we owed but could not pay.

The Bible tells us the story, history attests that it's true, and our spirit rallies to the news of a Savior! This is what Christians believe. We place our faith in a risen Savior for the forgiveness of our sins.

What Does It Mean to Be Good?

The second part of the question is equally as important. To understand what it means to be good, we need a baseline of comparison. In most cases, we consider ourselves a good man if we're better off than we were growing up and if we achieve as much if not more than our peers. This is a relative type of goodness, and it's not without merit. In this sense, you can be a good man without being a Christian.

However, I believe a man who follows Christ will experience this alongside the High Call God has placed on his heart. You see, our view of goodness is constrained by our view of the world. Without Christ there will always be an important page missing from our understanding of who we are and what this life is all about. With Him, the story begins to make sense. We see our part in it, the calling is heard more clearly, and we are empowered to be the men we are called to be.

This empowering comes about both supernaturally and practically. Supernaturally, we are adopted as sons of God. Practically, however, we experience the forgiveness of sin and shame. The root cause of most negative family dynamics is bitterness associated with unforgiveness and shame. Carrying these wounds of the heart often prevents us from being the good men we long to be. A belief in Christ invites healing into generational wounds and allows us to be better than we would be otherwise.

Profess Christ—A Simple Prayer

This is an unplanned section in my writing, but I feel compelled to include a simple prayer of faith: a profession of Christ as your personal Savior. There's nothing special about these words. No doubt others have done a better job than I have in writing a profession of faith in Christ. However, God asks us to come to him like children, so the bar has not been set particularly high.

If you feel a stirring in your heart to get right with God, to feel a sense of peace that surpasses understanding, and to be more kind, brave, bold, and loving, read these words and profess them with your heart:

> "God, I believe. I believe you know me and that you see me. You and I both know that I'm not the man I want to be. I have fallen short of who you want me to be. I've sinned in so many ways and I want you to know that I'm sorry. I believe that you love me and that your son, Jesus, died on a cross for me so that I could be forgiven of my sins, and so I could know you as my father. I thank you for my salvation in Jesus, and I give my heart to you from this moment forward.
>
> Please do a good work in me and help me heed the High Calling you have put on my heart.
>
> Remind me often of the good you see in me, and that you are proud to have me as your son.
>
> Amen."

Welcome to the family! Can you do me a favor? If you said this prayer and became a follower of Jesus, would you let me know? I want to celebrate with you!

THE CHURCH FAILS MEN

There is not enough of effort, of struggle, in the typical church life of today to win young men to the church. A flowery bed of ease does not appeal to a fellow who has any manhood in him. The prevailing religion is too comfortable to attract young men who love the heroic.

JOSIAH STRONG, AMERICAN EDITOR, AUTHOR, AND CLERGYMAN

From our earliest years, many men have bucked against the box that we're constantly told to be comfortable in. Ride on the school bus, but don't get too rowdy. Sit in class and be still and listen. Raise your hand if you have a question. Stand quietly in line for lunch. Recess is twenty-five minutes, not four hours. Let's all stay inside for the rest of the day. Here's a cubicle for you to do your work. Attend these meetings, but don't speak out of line. Come, listen to a sermon but don't ask any questions or have any dialog with others, inside, quietly.

I'll make a confession here that is a shared sentiment I've heard from dozens of men over the years: church sucks. It's boring, institutionalized, sterilized, sanitized, repetitive, effeminizing, impersonal, judgmental, and cliquish. There are no doubt churches that break from the traditional mold, but for many of us, the typical church structure is not a good fit. Many men who can connect with Christ can't imagine themselves ever connecting with a typical church.

For starters, men have far greater connections with God in the out of doors than they do within the confines of a building. Open air, open hearts, open minds—we're after something wild, not tamed. There is something more real about nature that we miss within the confines of a building and structured worship. Thought and movement are inseparable brothers for the conditioning of men. This isn't to say that men can't experience a connection with God within the walls of a church, but it often feels stifling. Yet again we're asked to follow a set of rules, and then watch as a Sunday morning service unfolds with set moments of predictable participation.

For men to grow we need engagement. We need to challenge and be challenged. We need a band of brothers that have our six, coaches and counselors, and life shared within a community of believers and non-believers alike. We need less comfort and more disruption. We desire to put our boots on and step into the muck of the world, to engage with the enemy, to feel passionate about a movement, and to live with purpose.

Call men to a passionate and sacrificial quest with the odds stacked against us, and you can't keep us away. Ask us to come calmly into a well-oiled, sterilized environment to sing songs about love, rivers, and oceans, and we can't wait to leave.

Most Pastors Don't Represent the Men We Want to Be

Modern pastors are cut from a unique stock. On the one hand, they excel at compassion and care. They are models of sobriety and calm. They are often even-tempered, considerate, community-oriented men with a proper haircut, a beautiful wife and family, and manners any mother would love.

While these are all imitable qualities, they are a far cry from the biblical examples set by a wandering carpenter, a traveling tent-maker, or weatherworn fishermen. Men are looking for genuine—not perfect—men to follow. The life a pastor leads is rather unrelatable to that of the typical working man. Pastors feel this as well, so they surround themselves with church-minded folks. That further ostracizes them from the company of the average Joe. As happens too often with those in the role of a teacher, pastors can gravitate towards the heady and miss out on the hands-on aspects of life. Yet, this is precisely where most men live or desire to live.

Men are typically drawn to the story and life of a missionary more so than a preacher. We want to follow the man who knows hard work and frequently puts himself into unpredictable situations. Too often, the Sunday morning preacher is soft and settled. The fight has left him. He may be tenderhearted and good at delivering a speech, but the fire that a man should have about himself has been reduced to a mere flicker. He has traded wrench turning for page turning. It would be better that he took up one without forgoing the other.

This is a generalization. But it's also a stereotype that's been earned over time.

One of the challenges is that church isn't just for men. It's for women and families as well, so we need a solution that works for everyone. I believe the solution is simple, yet bold and messy at the same time. We need smaller groups, smaller buildings, more lay preachers, and peer-led discussions. We need fewer service projects and more community projects and evangelistic opportunities.

I'd rather see a church build a theatre or a stage than add another wing to an already oversized building or hire yet another pastor. Many would be deeply impacted by having a Christian give a class on woodworking or beekeeping or art more so than a Sunday morning sermon. So much goes into the coordination of the weekend service that we miss opportunities to show up in the everyday, epic mundane. As a Christian, life looks different because we look at life differently.

The Christian life can't be experienced at a church service in the same way it can be when we're out of our element and mixed together with our neighbors. If we were to move in this direction, pastoring would be more of a role than a title. Men may listen to the pastor preach, but we would also have opportunities to be mentored by and form friendships with other men from the church in a more natural setting. We would be engaged in doing work that is important to the families of our community—both those who attend church and those who don't.

THE MANLINESS OF CHRIST

In the mid-1800s it was noted that young Christian men lacked the masculine vigor so readily apparent in their forebears. Not only were they physically unfit, they were also timid towards life. They had egos that were too fragile to be the bold and daring witnesses for Christ of the next generation. Many of the boys recognized this within themselves and looked to well-known heroes outside of Christianity for examples to imitate. While young men have always sought out heroes, the real concern was that they did not regard Jesus as a masculine hero they could look up to. Rather, they saw him as a gentle, passive, and quiet figure of religion.

Unfortunately, we are seeing this in our own age.

Men are seeking out examples of masculinity, but they don't see Christ as being the highest form of manhood. Much of this is due to the lack of masculine qualities demonstrated by the men of the modern church. The man with a warrior fire and spirit, who calls other men to action, is hard to find. In his place are the good-hearted men of genteel nature, a loose handshake, and a soft spine. To its peril, the church spends too much time trying to douse the sinful qualities of mankind and not enough time stoking the courageous and compelling fire of manhood.

Perhaps you've experienced this yourself. There is something in the story of Christ that draws you to Him, but when you meet Christians you don't feel as though you have experienced Christ. Too often within a church community we can feel an inhibition to be authentically masculine. Instead, we're asked to be more emotionally sensitive than mission aware. There's no doubt a balance to be struck here, but let us always look to Christ as the example we are working to live by.

In response to the unmanly youth of the 1800s, a movement was born called Muscular Christianity. It had many proponents, including Theodore Roosevelt who often spoke against the "doctrine of ignoble ease" and "the man of timid peace." He called for men to live the "strenuous life" and to "dare mighty things." The clarion call for a revival of manliness in the Christian church was taken up with fervor.

Scottish-born Alexander Maclaren was a Baptist minister who preached during the heyday of Muscular Christianity and knew something of the manliness of Christ. His sermons and expositions of Scripture have some of the greatest callouts of Jesus's manly traits I've read. I'll leave off this section with his thoughts on the matter.

> We are far too much accustomed to think of our Saviour as presenting only the gentle graces of human nature. He presents those that belong to the strong side of our nature just as much. In Him are all power, manly energy, resolved consecration; everything which men call heroism is there. 'He steadfastly set His face.' And everything which men call tenderest love, most dewy pity, most marvellous and transcendent patience, is all there too. The type of manhood and the type of womanhood are both and equally in Jesus Christ; and He is the Man, whole, entire, perfect, with all power breathed forth in all gentleness, with all gentleness made steadfast and mighty by His strength. 'And he said unto me, Behold the lion of the tribe of Judah. And I beheld, and lo, a lamb!'—the blended symbols of kingly might, and lowly meekness, power in love, and love in power. The supremest act of resolved consecration and heroic self-immolation that ever was done upon earth—an act which

> we degrade by paralleling it with any other—was done at the bidding of love that pitied us. As we look up at that Cross we know not whether is more wonderfully set forth the pitying love of Christ's most tender heart, or the majestic energy of Christ's resolved will. The blended rays pour out, dear brethren, and reach to each of us. Do not look to that great sacrifice with idle wonder. Bend upon it no eye of mere curiosity. Beware of theorising merely about what it reveals and what it does. Turn not away from it carelessly as a twice-told tale. But look, believing that all that divine and human love pours out its treasure upon you, that all that firmness of resolved consecration and willing surrender to the death of the Cross was for you. Look, believing that you had then, and have now, a place in His heart, and in His sacrifice. Look, remembering that it was because He would save you, that Himself He could not save. Maclaren, A. (1872). Sermons preached in Union chapel, Manchester. United Kingdom: Hodder and Stoughton.

A DREAM OF MY FATHER

As I was writing this chapter, I had a vivid dream that struck a chord in me. I shared it with my wife, Summer, and she encouraged me to share it with you. She's good for things like that. Plus, she's a straight up fox and those two things make for a good woman!

I don't know what this dream means or if it will mean anything to you. I don't suppose it to be a prophecy or anything of that sort, but I do feel it's both personal for me and, at the same time, meant to share.

In the dream, I'm walking through a building of some kind. There is a church service happening inside, but I'm making my way outside. My dad is there. He is older—probably the same age he was when he died—but this was my dad as he could have been had he taken a different path in life. He was sober and healthy looking, though still short and somewhat round. He was full of joy, and I could tell he felt as though he really belonged there.

Dreams are strange. You move through the dream world in a way that you can't in reality, yet you don't really pick up on it until the dream is over. As we made our way outside, I heard people singing. There were a number of friends who were sitting under a portico—that's a fancy word for a porch—and singing, and my dad and I were singing along. He was passing out some song sheets and making conversation as he did so.

I sat down on the front row and joined in the worship. I wish I could remember the song, but in the dream, I knew it by heart. My dad hopped back a row and handed out some sheets as he talked to someone. It was then that I noticed he had teeth. In the real world he had lost his teeth, which made him look even worse for wear. But here in the dream, he was smiling.

And this is the part that really touches me as I think on it. It almost brings me to tears as I write this. There was an empty folding chair next to mine. It was green like the rest of them. I looked at my dad and tapped on the empty seat so as to say, *"Come sit next to me."* He smiled and let me know that he would be there. I don't know why that impacts me so much except to say that I felt like a child in that moment, but it felt right to feel like a child with my dad.

I miss my dad, but I think most of all I miss the version of him that could have been. I had a glimpse of a different reality, and it was just about perfect. He was still himself in many ways and I knew, in the dream, that he still had a history with alcohol, but he had overcome whatever real-life demons had kept him bound. And, it had something to do with Jesus.

Just before I woke up, I looked off the fancy porch area and saw some people and their kids playing in a pool. All of this was happening at the same time—the service, the singing, the playing. I can't imagine this working in reality, but perhaps it could. Or, maybe it's a glimpse of how things will be. Like I said, I don't know the purpose behind the dream, but I do believe it's something to share with you and something to capture here so that I might be reminded of it years from now.

FINAL THOUGHTS

The flame we've been talking about—the fire that burns within you—is an eternal flame. The High Call we feel on our heart is placed there by God to draw us to Himself. It's a call to awaken us to the grand reality of which we are a part. It's a call to fully ignite our hearts and to live our lives as men. To do so, we must acknowledge the spiritual aspect of who we are.

When the final span of our life has been measured out, weighed, and set before us, and we think back on our life and what it meant, with all of the what-ifs and regrets, we can either face that moment with fear of the unknown, or the peace of going home.

If we've gotten to know Jesus Christ and put our faith in him, when those regrets and doubts and fears begin to creep up, we can hear him saying, "*It's all good brother. You're with me.*"

CONCLUSION

A FIRE WORTH TENDING

The most powerful weapon on earth is the human soul on fire.

FERDINAND FOCH, SUPREME ALLIED COMMANDER OF WORLD WAR I

I must have been ten years old, but the memory feels as though it happened yesterday. I had lost track of time and stayed later than expected at my friend's house. As I started to leave, I took one look out the door and saw how dark it had become outside. I lived with my grandparents, deep in the country on the edge of a river. My friend and I spent most of our days making up stories about aliens and ghosts, oftentimes convincing ourselves of the tales we spun. This was easy to do in a landscape so readily set to the scene of horror or adventure. Although the span between my friend's house and ours was only a tenth of a mile, to a ten-year-old boy with an active imagination, it was a black chasm of certain death.

I called my granddaddy to ask him to swing by and pick me up. When he asked me why I didn't just walk home, I explained that it was too dark. He responded by letting me know that he would not be coming to get me, and then hung up the phone.

I was afraid of the dark. I was afraid of the imaginary creatures and the stories I had created in my head to fill the void of the unknown.

Thankfully, I was also embarrassed and didn't want my friend to know just how terrified I was. I don't know how long I stood there staring out that door into the black abyss of night, but after some time I took up my courage and darted out the door.

I ran so fast that I barely felt my feet touch the ground. I ran barefoot over yards and gravel driveways. I leapt across ditches that I knew were there, not by sight, but by memory. I flew into the house, panting and heaving and filled with the exhilaration of having just cheated death.

In addition to the rush of adrenaline, I felt something else: pride.

I've often retold and thought back on this story over the years. It's a fun story and many people can relate to it, but it's not that different from the darkness we face as men. The fear of running into the night as a boy is similar to the feeling we have when we explore the untouched caverns of our souls as men. We often do it afraid, but do it we must.

You and I are brothers in the battle of our age. We are at war with complacency, ambivalence, abdication of responsibilities, anxiety, and those hell-bent on the eradication of anything resembling traditional, whole, healthy, and authentic masculinity. One of the greatest weapons we have is a man living his life deliberately and with the courage to earnestly tend the fire God has placed within his heart. We need men who are willing to go into the caverns of their own souls and discover the goodness that is hidden there. We need men who are willing to burn brightly and inspire others to tend to the flame of their own spirits. If you've read this book, I believe you want to be counted among such men.

As do I.

The willingness to take the next step on your journey to manhood begins with a belief that your fire is worth tending. It is, brother! Believe it! You are needed.

The logical next question is, "What now? How do I take the lessons in this book and apply them to my life?" Here are a few steps to get you headed down the right path.

STEP 1: GET A VISION

The High Call on each man's life contains unique elements suited just for him. God is good like that. You and I share in some of the broad aspects all men are called to, but your life will look different from mine. Make getting clarity on your life a priority. Asking the following questions can be helpful:

- What unique talents do I have?
- What am I drawn to?
- What would I want my grandchildren to say about me?
- What fears keep me from enjoying relationships to the fullest?
- What vision of the future sets my soul on fire?
- What vision of my future scares me?

STEP 2: MAKE A PLAN

Visions are great, but they don't get us where we want to go. A man with a vision for his life and no plan to get there will end up more disappointed than the one who never dared to dream.

There are a few non-negotiables that must be in your plan to succeed in becoming the man you long to be.

1. **A band of brothers**—Men who will inspire you, see the best in you, and also call you out when you start down a

bad road. See Stephen Mansfield's excellent book on the subject, *Building Your Band of Brothers.*

2. **Measure success in lives changed**—This of course includes yours but don't get caught in the trap of living solely for yourself.

3. **Be radically honest**—If you're not honest about what you want, where you are, and what's keeping you from where you want to be, you won't be able to progress.

4. **Small steps lead to big wins**—Don't get too ahead of yourself. What are the immediate things you can do to get headed in the right direction?

STEP 3: DO THE WORK

Most of the work that needs to be done is within ourselves, facing our fears and discomforts head on. Do the work of healing the wounds of your heart. Make amends where you can. Forgive and enjoy being forgiven. Exercise, eat to live, journal, give thanks, and be intentional about your life. Beyond these things, you will need to determine what a successful day and week look like for you.

This is where your band of brothers comes in. Make your daily and weekly non-negotiables known and be honest if you aren't measuring up. We all get off track and shift our priorities around in order to manage the things life throws at us. But the man who succeeds recognizes this and realigns himself with his goals.

God has started a good work in us, and He tends to see it through to completion. I'm glad to have you with me on this journey.

TEND YOUR FIRE.

ACKNOWLEDGEMENTS

To be completely honest, this is the one part of the book I feel the most incapable of doing justice. In one sense, I am thanking those who have helped me through the process of writing this book, but in a larger and more true sense, I am showing sincere appreciation for those who have made an impact on my life as I strive to make an impact on others. For such things, there are not words enough. However, shared commissions on this book are also out of the question, so words will have to suffice.

I want to first thank my wife, Summer. This book has been a long endeavor, and over the many years to its completion we have shared in some blessed times as well as some very trying times. She is without a doubt the toughest woman I know. This book would not be worth writing if not for the lessons we learned together. Thanks, Love!

There are several men in the movement to uphold masculinity in its truest and noblest form for who I am thankful. John Eldredge comes to mind first. His book, *Wild at Heart,* changed my direction in life. He was the first to show me the power of an author to speak so completely to the heart of another man. Thank you, John!

A big thanks to Stephen Mansfield for his steady, fatherly demeanor and heart for men, and his heart shown to me in particular.

Ryan Michler, thanks for your focus and passion in your mission with Order of Man, but more importantly, with your family. Many men are watching, and you lead by example.

To my editor, Brian Voss, you helped make this book so much better. Thanks for your perspective and willingness to be part of this project.

Lastly, I want to thank the men of Wolf & Iron, particularly those who have been part of this mission for so many years. Your continued engagement, support, and encouragement make this endeavor so worthwhile. There's more to come, fellas, and I'm glad to have you with me!

FIRE TENDING RESOURCES

Here are a few of my favorite books and podcasts for growing as a man. However, this list is constantly growing. Find a list of the latest manly resources at https://wolfandiron.com/resources.

BOOKS

Wild at Heart by John Eldredge

Sovereignty by Ryan Michler

Men on Fire by Stephen Mansfield

The Leap of Your Life by Tommy Baker

12 Rules for Life & *Beyond Order* by Jordan Peterson

Scary Close by Donald Miller

The Manliness of Christ by Thomas Hughes

Every Man a King by Orison Swett Marden

Fortitude by Dan Crenshaw

Mere Christianity by C.S. Lewis

Extreme Ownership by Jocko Willink and Leif Babin

The Obstacle is the Way by Ryan Holiday

Atomic Habits by James Clear

Staring Down the Wolf by Mark Divine

PODCASTS

Wolf & Iron—Mike Yarbrough

Order of Man—Ryan Michler

The Art of Manliness—Brett McKay

Danger Close with Jack Carr—Jack Carr

The Pursuit of Manliness—Jarrett Samuels

Unashamed with Phil & Jase Robertson—Phil & Jase Robertson

Jocko Podcast—Jocko Willink

The Dad Edge Podcast—Larry Hagner

ABOUT THE AUTHOR

Having spent his formative years on the banks of the Hatchie River in the small town of Mercer, TN, Mike Yarbrough yearns for the hardihood and old-school wisdom so common in generations past.

He is the founder of **Wolf & Iron** (https://wolfandiron.com) and **Rustic and Main** (https://rusticandmain.com)

Mike has a passion for entrepreneurship, stories, and helping men heed the High Call of manful living.

He now resides in Charlotte, NC with his lovely wife and two handsome sons.

photo by Seth Snide

Wolf & Iron

LIKED THE BOOK? JOIN THE MISSION!

WOLFANDIRON.COM/TENDINGTHEFIRE

CONNECT WITH MIKE AND OTHER MEN HEEDING THE HIGH CALL ON THEIR LIVES.